DEFINING DRUGS

Richard Henry Parrish II

DEFINING DRUGS

How Government Became the Arbiter of Pharmaceutical Fact

Transaction Publishers
New Brunswick (U.S.A.) and London (U.K.)

Copyright © 2003 by Transaction Publishers, New Brunswick, New Jersey.

All rights reserved under International and Pan-American Copyright Conventions. No part of this book may be reproduced or transmitted in any form or by any means, electronic or mechanical, including photocopy, recording, or any information storage and retrieval system, without prior permission in writing from the publisher. All inquiries should be addressed to Transaction Publishers, Rutgers—The State University, 35 Berrue Circle, Piscataway, New Jersey 08854-8042.

This book is printed on acid-free paper that meets the American National Standard for Permanence of Paper for Printed Library Materials.

Library of Congress Catalog Number: 2002075086
ISBN: 0-7658-0189-2
Printed in Canada

Library of Congress Cataloging-in-Publication Data

Parrish, Richard Henry.
  Defining drugs : how government became the arbiter of pharmaceutical fact / Richard Henry Parrish II.
      p. cm.
    Includes bibliographical references and index.
    ISBN 0-7658-0189-2 (cloth)
      1. Pharmaceutical policy—United States. I. Title.

RA401.A3 P376 2003
353.9'98'0973—dc21   2002075086

To Mary Almira Parrish, R.N. (1872-1950),
my great-great aunt, one of the first registered nurses
in the state of West Virginia, who homesteaded 400 acres
in the Wyoming plains (1920-1923), and is buried in the
family's Humphrey cemetery on deeded land
of the Northwest Territory

Contents

Figures

Foreword

Reading Richard Henry Parrish's detailed review and analysis of the interval between the 1906 Pure Food and Drug Act and the 1938 Food, Drug, and Cosmetic Act and its reverberations through time, prompts a dilemma. Are these laws the manifestations of calculations which enabled the growth of federal powers and enfeebled the will of individuals, or are the laws a formalized expression of the social contract among the citizenry of an increasingly complex society?

Rugged individualists may peel back the layers of regulations spawned by the two laws to reveal the machinations of populists who would encode a rational (read righteous and external) approach into the present and future of pharmaceutical development, marketing, and application. Each replication of the drug evaluation process therefore invites more governmental intrusion, with its attendant abridgement of individual rights and ultimate restricted access to potentially beneficial therapeutics. For readers of this mind-set, Parrish's book is a cautionary tale.

Readers who invest more trust in the promises of collective action under the guise of public beneficence are likely to view the two laws as the foundations of an ongoing success story—if not of better living through chemistry than of better living through the sharp observation and regulation of chemists. After all, the federal institution empowered by the two laws, The Food and Drug Administration (FDA), has adequately protected the populace from the corrupt (be they peripatetic charlatans or seemingly stolid corporations); the harmful (FDA delays minimized the impact of thalidomide in the U.S.A.); and near-do-wells (in the form of FDA recalls of diabetes drugs that poisoned livers and weight loss drugs that damaged hearts). Some would argue that the FDA's most dramatic accomplishments (and most threatening intrusions) lie ahead: absorbing full oversight of nutritional supplements and herbal remedies and revoking the privileges of tobacconists.

Each reader must pursue for himself the answer to the dilemma. Fortunately, Parrish has provided all the necessary clues for the pursuit. He also has rewarded the reader with precise descriptions and explanations of the personal and professional motives of the agents for change in the regulation of drugs and therapies, by tracing their tentative steps in defining a rational governance of pharmacotherapy, and their bold strides in erecting a durable apparatus that persists as one of the most formidable institutions of government.

Those readers who practice the healing arts will find answers to questions that they never thought to ask themselves. What are the boundaries of my practice? Who selected or mandated my professional limitations? What lies beyond the therapies available to my patients? Or simply, why do I practice the way I do?

The seeds of the health professions were planted centuries ago in the simple relationships that develop between the well and the ill. From these relationships some stratification of care sprouted, but not since the era of the guilds has professional behavior been as cultivated as during the few decades between the enactment of the 1906 "Wiley Act" and the 1938 Food, Drug, and Cosmetic Act. It was during these thirty years that physicians fully separated from pharmacists; that the activities of each profession were officially codified; and that physicians grasped prescription pads while pharmacists taped no trespassing signs over dispensing counters.

Though both laws responded to conditions in the first half of the twentieth century, it was not until the second half of the century that practitioners felt a substantial impact on practice style. Practice variation, long glorified and used to attract bright and independent students to the professional fold, appeared sacrosanct throughout the century. However, wide differences in approach (and results) were discussed as practice pollutants in the late 1800s. It took another century of appeals to validity and reproducibility to begin to topple personal testimonial from the pinnacle of medical knowledge. The battle between standards of practice and standards of reason has only grown more heated in the twenty-first century. Whether from governmental intervention, professional evolution, or individual responses to uncovered knowledge, the once wild rivers of practice style (based upon Victorian self-righteousness, organolepsis, or blissful ignorance) are being dammed, their meandering banks replaced with concrete culverts, their flow filtered through advocacy campaigns and political opportunism. The residual trickles are channeled into the modern constrained practices of medicine and pharmacy.

Safety has bumped style from the sacristy. We have become accustomed to the restrictions on our professional activities, yet Parrish compels us to take notice of the capitulation. Further, he provokes us to ask, "Are our privileges becoming more circumscribed? Are the walls closing in?"

Foreshadowing the scope of practice limitations, and by extension the erosion of an individual's access to drugs, may provoke groups interested in repealing federal powers. However, weakening governmental controls would do little to impede detrimental external influences on professional practice. Indeed, removing the modicum of protection that agencies such as the FDA exert while under congressional siege to be more responsive to special issue pleas and corporate constituents would create a power vacuum. Marketplace idealism suggests that individual oversight and choice would adequately substitute for the FDA. However, a comparison with nations that forego the functions of pharmaceutical definition, evaluation and verification provides an alternative scenario: private oversight is readily corrupted, privateering and adulteration of drugs is rampant, and individual choice is little more than a blind gambit.

As a practicing physician, who is also responsible for the education of physicians and pharmacists in training, my concerns lie more with insidious alterations in professional values. These alterations result less from threats from an imposing public institution than from the constant barrage of commercial advertisements, medical education sponsorships, and stealthy trysts among professional societies and pharmaceutical manufacturers. These covert and pervasive relationships induce us to convert life's slightest challenges into formal medical diagnoses and opportunities for peddling marginally effective, yet highly expensive, pharmaceuticals. Too often, it seems the culmination of medical practice is translating sniffles into allergic rhinitis and an episode of the blues into acute prozac deficiency.

Rather than exerting professional judgment and values, physicians and pharmacists have stood by while the public, primed by direct-to-consumer broadcasts, clamors for ever-increasing quantities of drugs. Complacent with a pass-through or middle-man role in the commerce between corporations as health care providers and patients as customers, the health care professions have been all too willing to abrogate their defense of the social contract that for centuries has guided the sick and needy to the educated and able.

Richard Henry Parrish warns against the long and reaching arm of law, its effects on drug development and availability, and hints at its potential to shape the spirit of a people. He doubts the worth and stability of any actions compelled by the threat of physical force.

However, there are other forces at large that influence individual and public health. Comfort, ignorance, apathy—each tool has been employed for individual gain at the expense of another's rights. Since we cannot purify our motives, it is left to government, as the least biased of institutions and functioning with the consent of the people, to verify our actions.

Defining Drugs invites each of us to consider our responsibilities as individuals, members of professions, and contributors to society, to safeguard a social contract that pre-dates all formal forms of government and anchors the purpose of pharmaceutical regulations in optimizing the relationship between the well and the ill.

Peter G. Teichman

Preface

Montani semper liberi. The conflict of jurisdiction between state and federal governments is a major part of my cultural heritage. I was born in the boundaries of what was one of the original thirteen colonies that, during the Civil War, became the state of West Virginia. *Montani semper liberi:* Mountain men always free. I have expressed my views on freedom and liberty as well as the government's proper role in the economy of drug therapy in my profession's literature[1] and in the newspapers of Huntington and Charleston, West Virginia, where I lived between 1985 and 1990. In four bimonthly issues, I published a free newsletter that I distributed to 100 key intellectual and political leaders in the profession of pharmacy, illustrating the philosophical and practical consequences of the Catastrophic Coverage Act of 1988.

As a boy, I read Plato's *Republic* and about Aristotle's *Magnanimous Man.* As an adult, I read Ayn Rand's *The Fountainhead* and *Atlas Shrugged.* I earned the silver palm as an Eagle Scout. I studied pharmacy because I could combine three of my great loves: love of chemistry, love of business, and love of people. I have practiced pharmacy for over twenty years in seven different states—Ohio, West Virginia, Kentucky, Pennsylvania, New Jersey, Minnesota, and Virginia. I have consulted with pharmacists, physicians, nurses, and administrators in thirty others. I have practiced nutrition support pharmacy (a therapy designed for those unable to eat), which required individualized patient assessment, monitoring, and follow-up. I successfully argued a case of unlawful discharge of an employee before a Federal arbitrator from Cleveland, Ohio. I restructured a hospital department into a practice; with twenty physicians, started a new hospital; provided clinical leadership in the formation of a new company; and taught on the clinical faculties of six universities.

I caught all of my three sons at parturition, one at home with lay midwives (Richard III) and two in birth centers with a nurse midwife (Frank and Calvin).[2] I know what being free means.

My pre-disposition for patient-centered health practice and pref-
erence for government's very limited role in any practice follows
from my profound respect for laissez-faire, laissez-passer classical
liberalism. I believe that the proper protective role of a government
in a free society is two-fold: (1) to guard an individual's life and
property against foreign invasion and domestic aggression (military
and police); and (2) to arbitrate contract disputes between parties
(judiciary). The government of a free country has the exclusive exercise of retaliatory physical force. All who live therein choose to
give up physical force. I am suspicious of government because of
its primary coercive nature. Today, misapplied physical force or threat
of force by government in response to global or momentary inequities is one of the great tragedies of our age.

I am a capitalist in politics because, by strictly separating the government from the economy, peaceful coexistence through cooperation among people is possible. I believe that every person's life is an
end in itself, and each person must choose its course. Human history is our struggle to be free from compulsion: Culture is our achievement of history.

Notes

1.   Parrish II, 1985a; Parrish II, 1985b.
2.   Parrish II and Parrish, 1983.

Acknowledgements

There's a story in my family about Aunt Mary, the nurse to whom I have dedicated this book. She was the first daughter of Joseph and Lucy Humphrey Parrish, her father a Union corporal who survived the Second and Third Battles of Winchester during the Civil War. In fact, I write this acknowledgment on the very site where Joseph and his future brother-in-law, Frank Humphrey, were captured by the Army of Northern Virginia, and sent to a Richmond camp as prisoners of war.

After returning from homesteading in the Wyoming plains in the 1920s, my Aunt Mary lived on the Humphrey family farm, demarcated by Ross Run near the confluence of the Hocking and Ohio Rivers. "Auntie" had a variety of farm animals, including chickens. One day, my father came running to her house with one of those chickens perched on his head, pecking the daylights out of him. Auntie fetched her .22 rifle, at a distance of twenty feet shot the bird dead from his blond mop, had my dad pluck its feathers, and prepared the chicken for everyone's supper that night. "No hen's gonna do that to my Dickie, and live to squawk about it," she probably said.

I share this private family story because, while I was preparing my Ph.D. thesis at Minnesota, "Dickie's" younger brother was collecting stories like this about my family, stories that capture a sense of who we are from our surviving memories, documents, letters, and pictures. Working as we were, simultaneously but separately, I learned a very important lesson from him: The true power of history lies in the courage it gives us to act in the present day for a better tomorrow. Auntie knew this, too, I'm sure. Because of his work on our family's record, the strength I derived from it, and so much more, I will always be humbly grateful to my uncle, Robert Alfred Parrish.

* * * * *

This book is the summation of my journey into the history and culture of drug therapy regulation. For their guidance and insights, I thank Professors Joan Langlois, Thomas Szasz, Irving Louis Horowitz, and Peter Teichman: Joan, who has supported me throughout and thoroughly; Tom, who named the book, "Defining Drugs"; ILH, who believed in the value of the work; and Pete, who wrote the foreword. Over a two-year period, pharmacy director Wayne Wandmacher and colleagues listened to my discoveries, and facilitated a flexible practice schedule to enable me to earn a living at North Memorial Healthcare while I finished my thesis.

My Ph.D. adviser at the University of Minnesota, medical anthropologist Peter C. Morley, constantly encouraged me to think and write as if I were not a pharmacist. Medical historian Jennifer L. Gunn rekindled my interest in history, and provided many insights into the nature of the relationship of history and the social sciences on which to base my investigation. As practitioner colleagues, Linda M. Strand and Robert J. Cipolle often reminded me that something usable should be derived from my research. Attorney Robert J. Levy impressed upon me the importance of understanding the broader themes of culture as well as the "slippery slopes" of both law and history.

Other individuals provided invaluable assistance during the archival research. Many thanks to Professors Gregory J. Higby, Elaine C. Stroud, and Glenn A. Sonnedecker of the American Institute of the History of Pharmacy (AIHP) who listened to my proposal during three visits (March 23-25, 1999; June 22-28, 1999; October 11-16, 1999), and suggested potential sources available on the campus of the University of Wisconsin, Madison. I am grateful for the financial support I received from AIHP.

Pharmacist-historian George B. Griffenhagen provided access to the archives of the American Pharmaceutical Association during two visits to Washington, DC (July 1-3, 1999 and November 8-10, 1999), and directed me to important correspondence of the National Formulary Committee and James H. Beal.

Professor David Klaassen, research archivist of the Social Welfare collection at the University of Minnesota, directed me through American Social Hygiene Association (ASHA) correspondence and reports on quackery and drugstores regarding venereal disease.

On the advice of Food and Drug Administration historian John P. Swann, I contacted research archivist Marjorie Ciarlante at the National Archives in College Park, Maryland, who guided me through the complexities of the correspondence decimal filing system for Record Groups 16 and 88.

For their comments and suggestions, my thanks to Peter Barton Hutt, partner, law firm of Covington & Burling, Washington, DC; David Brushwood, Professor of Pharmacy Healthcare Administration, University of Florida; John A. Crellin, Professor of Anthropology, Memorial University of Newfoundland; Ray Kondratas, Historian, Smithsonian Institution; and Debora A. Rougeux, Reference Archivist, University of Pittsburgh.

At Shenandoah University Bernard J. Dunn School of Pharmacy, my thanks to my boss, Dean Alan McKay, for access to the very capable skills of Mary Beth Board, who collected for me the copyright permissions needed for the quotations found in this book, which follow. Quotations used in the book but not listed are considered to fall under the fair use guidelines of the copyright laws of the United States of America. I gratefully acknowledge the following publishers, authors, and publications for permission to use previously published and archival material:

Marks, H. M. (1997). *The Progress of Experiment: Science and Therapeutic Reform in the United States*, 1900-1990. Cambridge: Cambridge University Press, pp. 19, 21-2, 37, 40-1, reprinted with the permission of Cambridge University Press.

Morgan, H. W. (1981). *Drugs in America*. Syracuse, NY: Syracuse University Press, pp. 66, 74, 97, 105, reprinted with the permission of the publisher.

Kremers Reference Files A2: Beal, James H. Used with permission of the American Institute of the History of Pharmacy, University of Wisconsin School of Pharmacy, Madison, Wisconsin.

Higby, G. J. (1992). *In Service to American Pharmacy: The Professional Life of William Proctor, Jr.* Tuscaloosa: The University of Alabama, pp. 14-5, 25-31, 51, 63, reprinted with the permission of the publisher and author.

Reprinted by permission of the publisher from SCIENCE IN THE FEDERAL GOVERNMENT: A HISTORY OF POLICIES AND

Introduction

Drug-related morbidity and mortality are major societal problems that needlessly waste the livelihoods and resources of many people in the United States. Johnson and Bootman estimated that the annual cost of illness and death from prescription pharmaceutical therapy misadventures in ambulant patients is $77 billion.[1] Control of drugs, as both cultural phenomena and therapeutic modality, was a major thread of the federal government's social health and welfare fabric in twentieth-century America.[2] How and why government exerted this control through the exercise of police power directly relates to an idealistic social construction I call "pharmaceutical fact."[3] This social construction involved the interrelationships of interest groups voicing predominant philosophical, teleological, and existential meanings of drugs.[4] The purposes for, and consequences of, control can be traced from the surviving historical record, and were derived from what was held to be true about pharmaceuticals. A rather sobering statistic illuminates the importance of understanding the historical evolution of government control. Today in the United States, an executive of a national health maintenance organization has implicated the untoward consequences of prescription pharmaceutical therapy in the deaths of more of its members annually than from automobile accidents, alcohol and tobacco use, and guns, combined.[5] A comprehensive understanding of the phenomena requires that we examine the historical and professional polity through which drug-related morbidity and mortality became a cultural expression in post-industrial society.

What is Pharmaceutical Fact?

Pharmaceuticals have chemical, physical, biological, pharmacological, toxicological, therapeutic, and economical properties. Their therapeutics relate to disease preventative, curative, palliative, and/or arresting properties in humans and animals. Pharmaceutical fact describes a social conception of pharmaceutical therapy and its control in society. It is comprised of cognitions that derive, but develop a separate "existence," from the properties of these substances. The idea of pharmaceutical fact is adapted to pharmaceutical therapy from Durkheim's idea, social fact. To Durkheim, social facts emerge from collective elaboration and impose their existence on the individual to constrain action within the body of beliefs and sentiments of an average of members in a society.[6]

Pharmaceutical fact is a concept of consciousness that presumes, but does not necessarily relate entirely or directly to, the existential circumstances of objective reality. It is the result of a collective transfiguration of the physically perceived characteristics of these therapeutic agents into a polity (broadly, a social structure) for governing pharmaceutical therapy. Wiebe noted the intellectual influence of idealism on the social organization of federal bureaus.[7] Sustained regulation at the federal level codification from purity of drugs to safety of pharmaceutical therapy began between 1906 and 1938, or between Progressivism's "Wiley Act"[8] and the "brain trust" reformation of the New Deal.[9]

Pharmaceutical fact bursts forth when two or more parties negotiate a discovery about the physical constants and effects of chemicals on living organisms. A chemical substance is a drug when it can induce observable changes in the physiopathology of a known disease by preventing, curing, arresting, or palliating.[10] A drug becomes a pharmaceutical with the identification, purification, standardization, and mass production of proximate principles or active ingredients.[11] Professionals in the United States Pharmacopoeial Convention Committee of Revision (USPC), American Medical Association's Council on Pharmacy and Chemistry (CPC), and American Pharmaceutical Association's National Formulary Committee (NFC) actually voted on the accuracy and acceptability of research results regarding the physical constants of proximate principles.[12] When applied to living organisms, like humans, plants, and animals, a pharmaceutical becomes therapy.[13] Thus, pharmaceutical fact is a summation of knowledge of physical constants and the effects of pharmaceutical therapy on the survival and sustenance of living organisms.

Pharmaceutical fact also subsumes the respective roles of practitioners involved, such as medicine and pharmacy, relative to control of pharmaceutical therapy by the state. The long history of interaction and conflict between medicine and pharmacy has centered on scientific educational credentials, scope of state licensure, and sanctioned relationships with individual patients. Jurisdiction and harmonization of laws in matters of pharmaceutical fact are historical manifestations of state versus federal control of pharmaceutical therapy. The 1951 Amendments to the Food, Drug, and Cosmetic Act of 1938, known as Durham-Humphrey Amendments (DHA), established the statutory nature of prescription pharmaceuticals. ("Caution: Federal law prohibits dispensing without prescription.") The 1997 Food and Drug Administration Modernization Act replaced DHA. Today, the Department of Health and Human Services' Food and Drug Administration defines and approves a prescription drug as *pharmaceutical therapy* that bears the symbol, *Rx only*. *Rx only* is an approved pharmaceutical entity comprised of both the pharmaceutical and its labeling, not just the physical and chemical composition of the pharmaceutical itself. Prescription labeling is the legal definition of a pharmaceutical, and includes professional product literature and advertising in addition to the physical label affixed to a product.

Moreover, pharmaceutical fact involves the transformation of polity to policy (law and regulation), including the use of police power to monopolize pharmaceutical mass production and use. Levine and Reinarman illustrated this kind of transformation during federal prohibition of beverage ethanol sales.[14] While not a part of this social system between 1900 and 1940, pharmaceutical distribution evolved to include clinical experimentation, authorization for marketing, mass production (domestic and foreign importation), separate prescribing and dispensing processes, evaluation of clinical episodes and endpoints, and financing mechanisms through public taxation and private insurance, pharmaceutical benefit management, and price controls.

Durkheim distinguished two types of social facts: material and non-material.[15] While I do not subscribe to the dichotomy of material and non-material facts or to the idea of "social fact" per se, many intellectuals of the period did. What is important in this context is the identification of the motive power that propelled government control, not whether I agree with the ideas of the time. During the period between the first and second federal acts related to pharmaceutical therapy, the major intellectual debate among social scientists and policy makers centered on idealism versus pragmatism in philosophy, and rationalism versus empiricism in therapeutics.[16] Durkheim, Marx, and Weber were intellectual idealists. Their social theories greatly influenced many social ideologues, like Croly and Dewey, who argued for organized, scientific government planning over the spontaneous laissez-faire, laissez-passer of Mill, Bentham, and Spencer.[17] Only when the physical results of idealism lay slain on the battlefields of Europe in the First World War did American intellectuals begin to embrace pragmatic doctrines that were purported to elevate material existence.[18]

The dichotomy of the material and non-material also influenced ideas of commercial and professional activities in pharmaceutical therapy and pharmacy practice. To quote Sletten,

> Businessmen are expected to be self-oriented and could pursue economic advantage through price competition. Professional men, on the other hand, are required to be "other-oriented" and were restricted in the pursuit of individual economic advantage through price competition. The retail druggist is not only a small businessman, but also a pharmacist. Since a pharmacist's role is functionally related to that of the physician and has characteristics associated with professional roles, it seemed plausible that the "other orientation" of professional men might be related to the strong concern of the retail druggist's organization to eliminate, or greatly reduce, price competition as it affected the retail druggist.[19]

The use of drugs was the material means to therapeutic ends. As surgery and obstetrics became distinct specialties in medicine, pharmaceutical recommendation came to dominate therapeutic intervention by the general practitioner.[20] Arguments by physicians and pharmacists alike for the functional regulation of pharmacy continued throughout the nineteenth century.[21] However, when allopathic physicians employed pharmaceuticals as their primary therapeutic intervention, pharmacy groups began to lobby for greater government control.

I argue that pharmaceutical fact describes a negotiated reality (non-material fact). A social structure through law and regulation (material fact) articulated this conception of pharmaceutical therapy in society. Negotiation began with judicial verdicts[22] and professional democracy[23] (majority voting), and continued even when instrumentation[24] provided more accurate determinations of proximate principles.

Prior Historical Work

There have been many themes used to explain various phases of pharmaceutical therapy legislation by government officials, sociologists, historians, economists, political scientists, jurists, and, even, health care practitioners. The legislation and regulation of medicines are not new phenomena. Penn argues that it is 3,000 years old.[25] Jackson posited that lethal misadventures in pharmaceutical therapy in the United States—primarily affecting women and children—captured the attention of the public and government to propel almost unanimous legislative adoption by members of Congress.[26] Young attributed unsuccessful federal regulatory efforts to control patent medicines and health quackery until the early twentieth century to individualism and Jacksonian democracy.[27] Libeneau explained the beginnings of organized centralization of control by reference to economic pragmatism, capitalism, and the rise of pharmaceutical monopolies in the development of antitoxins by both government and commercial interests.[28] Temin asserted that pharmaceutical therapy legislation has been a "logical" progression, an incrementally evolving apparatus that institutionalized the customary behaviors of practitioners and patients.[29] Starr placed the emphasis on a rising medical hegemony and the medicalization of life to explain society's historical response in the form of regulation.[30] Silverman and Lee have argued that protection of the public's health and dangers to collective well-being caused by impure and substandard drugs are the major reasons for legislation.[31]

These explanations greatly aid our understanding of the ascension of health as an object of policy in the United States. However, the polity from which the policy came is missing in these discussions. Historically, drug therapy was frequently initiated by mothers (for their families) and by neighbors, not strictly by health professionals. Moreover, although chronologically detailed, none of these accounts provides documentation on the origins of cultural "control" mechanisms used to legitimize and institutionalize pharmaceutical therapy as a social phenomenon. Further, there is little attention given to the application of problem-solving, as such, which gave rise to and bonded scientific certainty with the evolving purposes of public administration through the federal bureaucracies.[32] Finally, none explains how and why police power was necessary to enforce the distribution and utilization of scientific discoveries (i.e., pharmaceutical therapy) other than to suggest that it just made sense.[33]

The major limitation of prior research is the separation of addictive and non-addictive substances. Federal drug law began to control narcotic and alcohol content labeling issues related to self-medication with patent medicines. Weatherford suggests a connection between worldwide drug control efforts (and the black markets they created) and deterioration of world currencies.[34] When this control was not possible, government and the professions cooperated to limit narcotic use only under professional guidance. Narcotic control in the Pure Food and Drugs Act of 1906 formalized the idea of "dangerous drugs" and provided a foundation for medicalizing future non-narcotic pharmaceutical use. The Harrison Anti-Narcotic Act of 1914 codified the personalized nature of a prescription, and made the possession and use of pharmaceutical therapy without a legitimate order a criminal offense. The importance of historical research in this context is to derive the basis of current social and cultural forces regarding pharmaceutical therapy regulation in what Szasz calls the "Therapeutic State."[35]

How did the United States federal government become the arbiter of pharmaceutical fact? Why was an arbiter of "fact" needed between "producer" and "consumer?" Did any branch of government predominate? What social forces between Progressivism and New Deal brought about federal control? Could the social construction have occurred without physical force? What political movements and sub-movements were operative, what were their premises and arguments, and what actions did they advocate relative to pharmaceutical therapy control? What effect did treaties and war or armed conflict have on galvanizing a domestic federal approach? What are the connections between public health movements and pharmaceutical therapy control?

Organization of Chapters

Chapter 1, "The Search for Order" provides an overview of the historical and cultural context of drug use between Progressivism and the New Deal.

The purpose of Chapter 2, "Pharmaceutical Fact," is to describe how standards (for the identification, purity, manufacture, labeling, safety, access to, and price of pharmaceutical products and their application to people—therapy) constituted the major device for negotiation used by physicians, pharmacists, pharmaceutical industry, and the federal government. A mixture of political patronage and professional democracy influenced this negotiation.

Chapter 3, "Letters between Leaders," discusses the transformation of professional polity into social policy through education and legislation. The purpose of this codification was to elevate the professional practices of "rank and file" practitioners in medicine and pharmacy.

The correspondence of two prominent pharmaceutical educators, James Hartley Beal and Edward Kremers, illustrates how their unique leadership abilities contributed heavily to professionalization of pharmacy through legislation.

"Dispensing Doctors and Counter-Prescribing Pharmacists" (chapter 4) examines professional tensions and conflicting views of pharmaceutical fact and professional propriety surrounding the practices of dispensing physicians and counter-prescribing pharmacists who treated patients with venereal disease. Discussed are the activities and interpretations of an outside observer, the American Social Hygiene Association, with reference to efforts by state and federal governments to control the incidence and prevalence of venereal diseases.

In Chapter 5, "Negotiating Reality: The Construction of Enforceable Pharmaceutical Standards," I trace the evolving arbiter role of the federal government through the Bureau of Chemistry (BOC) and Food and Drug Administration (FDA). Interaction between government (chemists, pharmacologists, and administrators) and private citizens in professional groups found in the general correspondence files of the BOC and FDA illustrates the influence of government over the writing of enforceable standards for pharmaceutical therapies.

In the conclusion, "Defining Drugs: The Consequences of Seeking External Governance," applies three themes from the period—"Rights and Responsibilities," "Reform," and "Definition of a Drug—Governmental or Cultural."

Notes

1. Johnson and Bootman, 1995.
2. Shorter, 1987.
3. Balandier, 1970; Skocpol, 1992; Bakalar, 1984.
4. Skocpol, 1992: 41.
5. Abate, 1999.
6. Durkheim, 1966:13; Marshall, 1994: 66, 486.
7. Wiebe, 1967 and 1975.
8. The "Wiley Act" is the Pure Food and Drugs Act of 1906 (Pub. L. 59-384); Anderson and Higby, 1995; Longest, 1998.
9. The Food, Drug, and Cosmetic Act of 1938 (Pub. L. 75-540) repealed the "Wiley Act"; Anderson and Higby, 1995.
10. Anderson Jr., 1958 and 1964.
11. Proximate principles are now called active ingredients. See Higby, 1992.
12. AMA Council on Pharmacy and Chemistry, 1916.
13. Rosenberg, 1979; Marks, 1997.

14.   Levine and Reinarman, 1991.
15.   Durkheim, 1966.
16.   Marks, 1997.
17.   Stieb, 1966.
18.   Hofstadter, 1955.
19.   Sletten, 1959:,4-5.
20.   Numbers, 1987.
21.   Higby, 1992; Kremers, 1940; Sonnedecker, 1986.
22.   Gates, 1934.
23.   Anderson and Higby, 1995.
24.   Higby, 1992.
25.   Penn, 1979.
26.   Jackson, 1970.
27.   Young, 1961: 44-74; Young, 1967: 18-20, 27-8.
28.   Libeneau, 1981.
29.   Temin, 1980.
30.   Starr, 1982.
31.   Silverman and Lee, 1976.
32.   Dupree, 1957: 256-301.
33.   Young, 1964: 217-9; Young, 1967.
34.   Weatherford, 1997: 207.
35.   Szasz, 1992.

1

"The Search for Order" between Progressivism and the New Deal

At the turn of the twentieth century, any American adult could trade for any purported medicinal product made by any manufacturer for any purpose from any party of their choosing.[1] Forty years later, an entire social system for drug therapy had developed to govern the identity, purity, labeling, manufacturing, safety, and access of products for pharmaceutical therapy. About academic and professional pharmacy during this period, Jackson noted: [2]

> The primary division [about legislation] was between the more professionally minded organizations, such as the American Association of Colleges of Pharmacy, versus the more commercially oriented groups, such as the National Wholesale Druggists Association. In general, the professional groups initially stood united with other drug interest in opposing the Tugwell bill. This soon changed. The American Association of Colleges of Pharmacy, the American Pharmaceutical Association, and organizations of similar type had a major interest in the scientific aspects of drugs as well as in public health. They were also interested in establishing pharmacy as a recognized profession. They were less concerned with the commercial side of the business and they were relatively immune to the pressures of the drug manufacturers.

Marks[3] addressed the influence of academic medicine:

> The standards of evidence articulated by the council were widely endorsed within academic medicine…. These standards formed the basis for federal drug regulation in the 1930s and 1940s.

Between Progressivism and the New Deal, self-medicating—an established cultural process of drug therapy in the United States—legally divided at the federal level into distinct, mutually exclusive domains: medical and criminal. As Bakalar surmised, "Drugs are symbols charged with cultural tensions."[4] He noted that the trend toward increased government control of all drugs rested on "authoritative knowledge about safety and efficacy."[5] Control came at a

1

particular developmental stage in American medicine and capitalist industrial society.[6] An evolving division of scientific medical labor directed the sacred and ethereal to legitimize and medicalize drug therapy. Alternatively, that considered profane and visceral came under the purview of an evolving state apparatus designed first to control non-medical drug use through taxation, then to prohibit and punish it through criminalization.

The executive branch firmly established the federal bureau system, especially the departments of Agriculture, Commerce and Labor, and Treasury.[7] The process of criminalization encroached into the medical sphere as government officials, professionals, industrialists, consumers, and the representatives of each negotiated the narrowing cultural scope of pharmaceutical fact.[8] This democratic winnowing of fact had a powerful influence on the standards of pharmaceutical therapy, and led to the development of one of the most financially successful endeavors ever known—the pharmaceutical industry.[9]

Empirical self-medicating with secret remedies had become a threat to public health, corporate profits, and national sovereignty.[10] Brandt noted the pervasive impact of nostrums as venereal disease treatments. The Surgeon-General's office could not even be sure of medicines used to treat venereal disease in soldiers.[11] As Brown pointed out, scientific medicine aided the achievement of corporate business goals.[12] Prevailing attitudes toward government intervention, for example, in New York State, illuminated the trend toward greater centralized control by either government or corporate interests.[13] The country needed narcotic control to regulate public access to mood-altering "dangerous drugs" as well as to comply with treaty obligations.[14] Self-selected medication use with secret formulas threatened the professional and commercial viability of pharmacy, medicine, and industry.[15] Morgan noted:[16]

> Commentators increasingly relied on metaphors drawn from bacteriology and public health.... The fear grew that [narcotic] drug use was a plague, a communicable disease for which there was no treatment except prevention. The growing sense that it was a national problem coincided with other forces that pointed toward regulation. The movement to control or outlaw undesirable behavior gained added force for being international.

Only medically directed pharmaceutical use—"rational therapeutics"—was considered appropriate for the citizenry by the federal government and corporate philanthropists. This was because, for the first time in history, pharmaceutical therapy began to demonstrate direct and predictable effects that could powerfully change the course of disease.[17] To quote Marks:[18]

> Circumstances called for a new attitude to replace the purported "therapeutic nihilism" of the early nineteenth-century skeptics: "rational therapeutics".... A rational, as opposed to an empiric remedy, was one whose effects were demonstrable in the laboratory and ideally one that acted on the cause, not the symptoms, of disease.

During the first third of the twentieth century, many social welfare activists, corporate philanthropists, and government officials thought that the complexities of life overwhelmed the abilities of ordinary citizens to make judgments regarding their therapeutic choices.[19] A number of factors supposedly led to this complexity. Medical and pharmacy professionals believed that patients were not competent to make judgments about whether a product was adulterated or misbranded for its intended use.[20] The development of an industry-based national economy provided a staggering variety of new products.[21] Illiteracy and "moral turpitude" of the citizenry was rampant.[22] The family unit was disintegrating because of migration from family farms to employment in urban factories.[23] The average citizen could not understand scientific discoveries and application of new theories of disease and individual susceptibility.[24] The secret formulas of patent medicines and nostrums threatened health and safety because no one, not even doctors and pharmacists, knew product constituents. As Simmons noted:[25]

> These medicines appealed to a certain class of doctors.... The fancy, catching names which caught the physician caught the layman as well, and the latter, finding not only full directions for use, but the names of the diseases in which the remedies were indicated, naturally bought them in reference to the so-called "patent medicines".... The physician became the unpaid peddler of secret nostrums; as the secret nostrum manufacturer became richer, the physician became poorer...but how is the physician to separate these preparations which are ethical from those which are not?

A constant barrage of inducements and promises from patent medicine makers as well as newspaper and circular advertisements from "health clinics," "physicians," "doctors," "reverends," "professors," and other "practitioners" manipulated individual behavior with regard to diabetes[26] and venereal disease[27] treatment as well as tobacco, narcotic, and alcohol abuse.[28] Many of these purveyors of nostrums understood the cultural nature of drug use.

The federal government justified constraint of individual choice by the founding tenets of federalism through its constitutional authority to regulate interstate commerce, taxation, and make treaties.

Figure 1.1
Timeline of Significant Events between 1900 and 1940

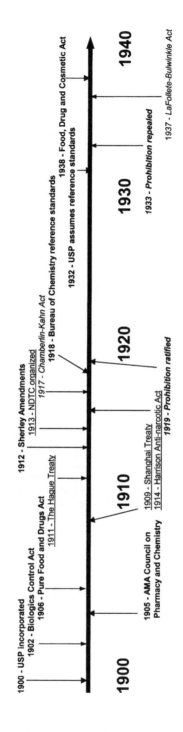

Legend:
Bold – drug-related event
Italic – Venereal disease-related event
<u>Underlined</u> – narcotic-related event
Bold italic – alcohol-related event

The charge of the federal bureau system was to protect the good of all citizens in an effort to "promote the general welfare." Moreover, conflicts of municipal and state level law made the individual's determination of medicinal value inefficient for business and the state.[29] According to Kremers:[30]

> The first desire for nationalization of American pharmacy came from the physicians. Whatever might be the lack of uniformity so far as the educational standards of physicians was concerned, the need for greater uniformity in medical preparations was felt at an early date.

Neither government nor business could legitimately address trade across state borders. AMA leaders like Simmons and Torald Sollman, a professor of pharmacology at Western Reserve University, held that the federal government should evaluate all new medical products.[31] Because of interstate commerce and international narcotic treaties, standards regarding the physical characteristics and therapeutic choice of drug therapy were believed to be unenforceable without the consistent threat and exercise of federal police power. Many occupational and professional groups organized for collective action during the period,[32] and lobbied at local and state levels for a variety of practice as well as food and drug laws.[33] Pharmacy practitioners sought state licensure to afford protection from the uncertainties of the market, and to differentiate themselves from physicians[34] whose major therapeutic intervention was drug therapy.[35] Protection from market uncertainty was related to both production and consumption of drug therapy. Many groups advocated for exclusionary-type legislation. Pharmacists sought to formalize a position as keeper of the drugs as well as arbiter of identity and purity. At the time of the 1906 Pure Food and Drugs Act, the physical standards of drug therapy preparation had been designed for small-scale, individual compounding of crude pharmaceuticals. To quote Higby:[36]

> By establishing and popularizing this process [of percolation], Procter sought to achieve several of his professional goals: to bring standardization to botanical drugs, to elevate the stature of pharmacists by improving the elegance of drug preparations, to keep the manufacture of drug preparations in the shops and out of large factories, and to ensure the quality of drug products and prescriptions for the public. Over time these goals varied in importance, but until his death Procter retained his faith that the full utilization of percolation would greatly enhance the progress of American pharmacy.

But, pharmacists did not want their practices limited to prescription referral only. By restricting who could produce, not who should consume, they could create a sustainable demand for professional services involving drug preparation. And, by 1940, pharmacists had become terminal distributors of finished dosage forms provided to them by a widely expanding scientific pharmaceutical industry, an industry whose major interest was influencing the legally endowed prescriptive power of the allopathic physician.

Over time, industry favored simplicity in distribution channels for drug therapy because it limited the expense of promotion to a mass audience and severed their linkage to "patent" medicine and nostrum makers, the targets of continuous legislative and media assaults.[37] At first, however, the industry sought direct communication with consumers; the AMA leveraged its position as arbiter of medical science to convince companies of its stewardship of therapeutics. As Marks pointed out:[38]

> Coincident with the development of national marketing of consumer goods, drug advertisers sought to bypass physicians as a source of therapeutic information and authority.

Industry efforts to channel their synthetic products to the prescriptions of informed intermediaries institutionalized the ideas of safety and "dangerous drugs."[39] Marks noted:[40]

> In the absence of reliable evidence, the council turned to reliable men. The opinions of experts were an imperfect substitute for facts, but their allegiance to science meant that they would only err. They would not deceive.... Belief in the integrity of scientists formed on part of the council's official pronouncements on experimental method, but where a particular truth could not be established, a proven dedication to truth might suffice. The assurance of reformers in the contributions of experimental method to medicine was premised on a relentless confidence in the future: truth will out.

Medical schools adopted a scientific curricular orientation on therapeutics away from materia medica by embracing experimental pharmacology and the laboratory sciences. Swann noted:[41]

> Pharmacology and chemistry were crucial to drug development in the period between the wars. Chemistry was important for synthesizing new drugs and isolating natural products such as insulin, liver extracts, and vitamins. Pharmacology was useful for designing new drugs for possible synthesis on the basis of anticipated therapeutic action and for testing experimental drugs in the laboratory. Chemistry and pharmacology were the most frequent foci of research interactions during this period.

The physician became a central figure in industry's efforts both to discover and expand products for and methods of drug therapy utilization. Again, Marks found:[42]

> Reformers accordingly pursued two related goals in the name of rational therapeutics. On the one hand, they sought to control the introduction and promotion of new drugs.

On the other, they attempted to foster a scientific and critical attitude toward therapeutics in the medical profession itself. The two reforms were interdependent. Restricting the number of drugs to a handful of proven remedies would lessen practitioners' confusion and thereby contribute to more "rational" therapeutic practice. At the same time, successful efforts to reform the industry depended upon the support of a reformed profession, one capable of recognizing the merits of using only carefully screened products.

Pharmacy curricular reform based on science lagged behind medicine. The National Association of Boards of Pharmacy (NABP)[43] and the American Association of Colleges of Pharmacy (AACP)[44] did not adopt a four-year bachelor of science in pharmacy as the entry-level degree required for licensure until 1932.[45] Jackson noted that AACP was very active in reform efforts of the 1906 Pure Food and Drugs Act.[46]

The function of pharmacy provided a necessary intermediary for the physician between medicine and chemistry, much like pharmacology was to the interface of medicine and physiology. Pharmacology had replaced materia medica as the root science of therapeutics in medicine although Marks noted:[47]

Successful therapeutic reform depended on changing physicians at the bottom, not the top, of the profession. For these physicians to change, medicine, no less than the market, had to be governed by science. Few physicians shared in the full strength of reformers' conviction that the future of therapeutic progress lay in the laboratory.

However, unlike physiologists who were instrumental in the development of pharmacology, the function of pharmacy did not have living organisms as its central focus. Pharmacists concerned themselves with the physico-chemical constants and standards of materia medica,[48] and conceded therapeutics to physicians.[49] While pharmacists did not want physicians in control of regulation or curriculum, many physicians (notably Albert Prescott at the University of Michigan) had been directly involved in academic training of pharmacists at universities.[50] Moreover, the American Medical Association (AMA) was a major contributor to passage of the 1906 Act in an effort to modulate the activities of manufacturing pharmacists. (Due to fear of "socialized medicine," AMA played a minor role in the 1938 Act.)

The validation of laws governing inanimate matter dominated pharmacy practice of the period, not the pharmacotherapy of patients. Through enactment of state laws on poisons, drug standards, and pharmacist qualifications through improved educational requirements, pharmacy leaders thought a uniform professional practice and standards of drug integrity would derive with minimal influence from commercial exigencies. As Higby noted, "Poisons and their improper handling created the loudest call from outside of pharmacy for increased regulation of the drug trade."[51] Kremers attributed the idea of state control to the influence of immigrant German apothecaries. [52]

> With the German revolution of 1848 this situation changed somewhat, since the great immigration movement from that country brought with it not a few well educated "Apotheker." These German apothecaries also brought with them the idea of a State control. Spasmodic efforts to control city druggists by local ordinances concerning the sale of poisons, if nothing more, had been made repeatedly, but did not prove very effective. The political corruption that permeated municipal government was not apt to produce good results.

After the 1906 Pure Food and Drugs Act, the courts decided the legality of descriptions on the label of a substance.[53] Many groups of pharmacy-trained individuals organized to negotiate the identity, purity, and uniform potency of medicinal agents. The United States Pharmacopoeia (USP) and the National Formulary (NF) became official standards of drug integrity as one result of the 1906 Pure Food and Drugs Act. In 1913, National Drug Trade Conference (NDTC) organized to address the practicalities of narcotic control.[54] Under the stimulus and leadership of Professor James H. Beal, the National Drug Trade Conference (NDTC)[55] brought together pharmacist organizations, such as the American Pharmaceutical Association (APhA) and the National Association of Retail Druggists (NARD), and ethical and proprietary manufacturers for the primary purpose of creating a unified front in response to narcotic control at the federal level. His successful effort to incorporate the USP and NF as the *only* official standards in United States law was unprecedented.[56]

Organized in 1888, the Committee on Unofficial Standards of the American Pharmaceutical Association (APhA) guided the work of the National Formulary.[57] The United States Pharmacopoeial Convention (USPC) Committee on Revision,[58] the American Public Health Association's Committee on Food and Drugs,[59] the American Medical Association's Council on Pharmacy and Chemistry,[60] and private non-profit corporate groups such as Francis Stewart's National Bureau of Materia Medica[61] and National Bureau of Medicines and Food[62] attempted to address drug constituent and therapeutic questions. AMA's *New and Nonofficial Remedies* provided practicing physicians with a listing of useful, non-proprietary preparations not listed in the USP. *United States Dispensary*, originated by physicians Wood and Bache of Philadelphia,[63] provided another compendium of drug standards for practitioners of both disciplines.

The federal government organized its efforts for drug control. The Department of Agriculture's Bureau of Chemistry established a Division of Drugs under the direction of pharmacist-physician Lyman Kebler[64] in 1907. At the same time, the Federal Specifications Board was organized with leadership from the National Bureau of Standards (1901) and the Association of Official Agricultural Chemists (1884).[65] Dupree noted:[66]

> The Bureau of Chemistry in the Department of Agriculture especially reacted, both because Wiley was trying to do chemistry for other agencies through his contracts laboratory and because pure-food-and-drug problems usually involved standards of purity and the like…. However, Wiley failed to show that the Bureau of Standards had any serious intention of taking over enforcement of the pure-food-and-drug laws or any extensive program in agricultural chemistry.

Many members of these professional groups were trained both in pharmacy and medicine, and held appointments and leadership positions simultaneously in multiple groups in and out of government. Gradually, as the institutional configuration of governing shifted from individual to collective organization and action, the cacophony emanating from private professional efforts to create enforceable standards resonated in the evolving structure of the federal bureau, especially in the Department of Agriculture. Professionals desired control of patent medicines because the products had secret formulas.[67] For many years, pharmacy leaders had been concerned about if and how to regulate the practice. William Proctor, the father of American pharmacy, returned from a trip to Europe convinced that governmental interference could benefit both the profession and the public. To quote Higby:[68]

> Procter came home with a different view of continent pharmacy than he had carried across the Atlantic in April. He had expected the International Pharmaceutical Congress to be an impressive forum for the exchange of pharmaceutical knowledge; instead he found delegates haggling over political issues. When pharmacy in the United States came under attack at the congress as an example of unregulated practice, Procter responded with a short address. Instead of defending the open competition that existed in American medical and pharmaceutical practice, he described the progress made in the previous fifty years and the prospects for the future. Procter kept his own personal opinions largely to himself and stuck to the facts as he saw them. In the midst of his address, however, Procter digressed to state that he favored a system that allowed only graduates of pharmacy schools to practice pharmacy, although such practice should be

subject to open competition. During his travels on the Continent he concluded that governmental interference could benefit both the public and pharmacists.... Before his trip to Europe, Procter rejected any suggested reforms or laws that could infringe on open competition or give too much power to the government.

German-born John M. Maisch had proposed a model pharmacy law in 1869 to provide a comprehensive approach to the physical products of materia medica, a unification of poison laws, and the regulation of qualifications and activities of pharmacists. King noted: [69]

> The report became the precursor of a "draft of a proposal to regulate the practice of pharmacy and the sale of poisons and to prevent adulteration of drugs and medicines," prepared by Maisch and a special committee, and presented at the next annual meeting [of APhA] (1869). Despite not having the Association's formal approval, this proposal was distributed to the legislatures and governors of each state, and became the basis of the first state pharmacy laws in this country.

But, owing to the nation's British roots, pharmacists were known in America during the time by many names, such as chemist, druggist, apothecary, and prescriptionist, with further differentiation as retail, wholesale, community, neighborhood, and dispensing. These multiple labels, often used rather whimsically, illustrate the fractional nature of a confused professional identity and the internal competition that beset the emerging discipline.

In urban areas, as pharmacy and medicine had separated into a specialized division of labor,[70] an educational vacuum was created as apothecaries and physicians were no longer serving apprenticeships in the dispensaries of the medical office. As Sletten observed:[71]

> In the nineteenth century when physicians were beginning to give up compounding and their open shops, the inadequate and variable training of druggists caused medical educators to propose that schools of pharmacy controlled by medical schools be established. The apothecaries in the few cities reacted by forming their own "colleges."

There were few enforceable standards for the identification, preparation, and sale of crude drug products, and no disclosure laws that would require the revelation of nostrum contents. AMA's Council on Pharmacy and Chemistry issued ten rules they required manufacturers to meet for listed products in their publication, *New and Non-Official Remedies*.[72] In addition to the physician and manufacturing pharmacists and chemists, these rules also pertained to the retail druggist. Secret formula or "patent" medicines (most had no government-issued patent) threatened the economic viability of both medicine and pharmacy. While professional associations for both disciplines had been established in the mid-nineteenth century, in part, to differentiate the genuine from quackery and charlatans,[73] a collateral concern continued to be the ability to make a good living from professional practice. Pharmacists insisted that physicians prescribe narcotics only after physical examination. As Musto found:[74] "Without such a provision, they feared physicians could set up narcotic dispensaries in their offices and 'prescribe' for all who came in." Professional and product standards were important ties to progressive reforms of the day. As Morgan noted:[75]

> Like druggists, physicians resented being identified with drug use and addiction. They also dreaded the record keeping, paperwork, and taxation that would follow regulation.... The AMA favored controlling habit-forming drugs and narcotics for both moral and practical reasons. Its most prominent spokesmen prior to the World War accepted the broad goals of the purity movement, linked drug addiction and abuse with unhappiness, inefficiency, and now crime. Medical spokesmen, like counterparts in pharmacy, saw the advantages of professionalization of being linked with progressive reforms. And they wished to eliminate the marginal doctors who gave the profession a bad name.

Organizationally and culturally, pharmacy manufacturers and practitioners alike found themselves situated between two cultural pillars—medicine, its functional root, and law, its perceived "professional" transformer.[76]

Patent Medicines and Self-Medication

Patent medicines clearly forced a distinction, perhaps an artificial one, between the professional and commercial interests of everyday practice as well as between physicians and pharmacists. As Higby noted: [77]

> Clashes between physicians and apothecaries did not occur commonly before the 1840s largely because apothecaries accepted their subservient position to the physician, and the number of drugstores, although on the rise, had not yet reached the saturation point. Feeling more confident of their standing, apothecaries began shifting their allegiance from physicians to their customers. Consequently, they took to refilling prescriptions without physician authorization, and to diagnosing and treating customers, a practice called "counter-prescribing."

In reality, nostrums were simply another choice of remediation in existence. These widely available home remedies, recommended by physicians and sold by them or in drug stores and through the mail, were not serving a socially acceptable purpose in the view of academic idealists and public welfare advocates. Morgan noted: [78]

> Most of the mail-order doctors followed procedures that allayed the patient's skepticism, fed his hopes, and made him seem important and unique. Each buyer filled out a

personal history, with attention to how long he or she had taken the particular drug, in what dosage, and with what effects. The vendor then appeared to tailor the compound for them. He encouraged the user to report on progress, and if "cured", to endorse the product. Many such testimonials were false, but most doubtless were genuine, written in the euphoria when the patient thought himself cured. Relapses were not recorded; nor were the users who became addicted to the nostrum…. The widespread sale of these compounds illustrated the extent of addiction and the effort of many people to seek anonymous cure.

Further, Musto pointed out "numerous patent medicines containing no more than the permitted amounts of morphine, cocaine, opium and heroin could continue to be sold by mail order and in general stores."[79] Many nostrums were thought to be both socially dangerous and personally addictive. Again, Morgan noted:[80]

By the turn of the century the sanitarium business was important. It was well organized, in the hands of acknowledged experts, and had many standardized procedures that allowed for individual variations. In some towns, the sanitarium tower rivaled the railroad station as a sign of progress. The movement testified to the organizational changes that had transformed the nation's medicine as well as its economy.

Both the labeling and advertising of remedies promoted the idea of self-directed therapy for many ailments without the benefit of educated, informed judgment from professionals.[81]

Partly in response to the secret formulas of nostrums and to the evolving success of experimental pharmacology, ethical pharmaceutical manufacturers began to capitalize on their position as a direct supplier to medical professionals of finished dosage forms of reliable and predictable composition and reproducible effects.[82] Pharmaceutical manufacturers created and expanded internal scientific research activities to support greater market penetration and dominance.[83] Many scientists throughout their careers alternated employment and consultancy roles between what Swann called the three estates of science: industry, academia, and government.[84]

The federal government's approach to patent medicine making—many products contained unlabeled opium and ethanol—was guided by many of these people who favored professionally sanctioned, non-commercial control of drug standards and production in response to the rising pressure of consumer-related interests and publicity surrounding the monopolistic practices of business. To provide insight into the self-observed character of Harvey Washington Wiley, BOC's first chief chemist, see the discussion leading, in his mind, to formation of the Referee Board of Consulting Scientific Experts (the "Remsen Board"). Why did Wiley seek out women's groups to enlist support for pure food and drugs?[85] Women did not have the right to vote, but Wiley knew that women were preparing food and medicine for family consumption that they did not produce themselves.[86] Moreover, women used patent medicines with greater frequency than men. As Musto noted, many "middle-class and middle-aged women from rural areas or small towns" were unknowingly habituated to opiate-containing nostrums.[87] Women were also the major purchasers of consumer goods in the new consumer economy.[88] Because of his evangelical background,[89] Wiley used a message of fear as he practiced his congressional testimony on unsuspecting social clubs.[90]

Pharmaceutical companies that refrained from communication with the public were called "ethical." The "ethical" pharmaceutical industry only advertised and distributed their products to professionals of their choosing. Restricted distribution created additional concerns among some pharmacists that would drive "restraint of trade" issues throughout the period ultimately leading to a monopoly on the dispensing of "legend" drugs. But, the industry was also the major source of patent medicine manufacturing,[91] providing the relabeler and wholesaler with ready made products.

Since exchange between patients and practitioners was modulated at the municipal or state level,[92] the federal government could only enforce legislation from organic acts that were constitutionally consistent with the principles of federalism—the commerce clause, taxation, and treaty making.[93] Drug law at the federal level could not have been approached at all without preceding acts on interstate commerce (1887) and anti-trust (1890). As Beal commented in 1895, the United States Constitution was not sufficiently robust to allow for federal control of drug therapy. However, quoting Young:[94]

> The temper of the times was changing. To protect the national health by a broad-gauge national law seemed less a violation of the Constitution than it once seemed.

Nevertheless, these two acts provided the institutional structure for enforcing the bureaucratic mechanisms of specific, commercial activity like drug therapy.

Only after the Pure Food and Drugs Act became law on 30 June 1906 could the federal government enter into treaties designed to control the international narcotic trade. At the time, America was the only Western country without domestic drug laws. American political leaders were desperate to "catch up" with the drug policing activities of Europe, especially those of Great Britain and Germany.[95]

What would be the domestic corollary to the Hague Convention? Fresh from the direct experience of martial law under Governor General William Howard Taft in the conquered Philippine Island archipelago, repatriated bureaucrats in the federal government knew firsthand the power and threat of narcotics for both subduing a population for military purposes, and maintaining a controllable workforce during peace. Narcotic trade could also generate internal revenue, a Taft idea borrowed from the British whose application to domestic control was vetoed by Theodore Roosevelt.[96] Culminating in the Harrison Anti-Narcotic Act in 1914 under Woodrow Wilson, however, bureaucratic control efforts were primarily designed to increase internal revenue by taxing medical narcotic possession and criminalizing non-medical possession and use by citizenry.[97] Medicine and pharmacy seemed to be concerned only with record keeping requirements and additional taxation. To quote Musto:[98]

> Eventually, a compromise permitted the physician to abstain from record keeping when out of his office, say at the bedside of an ill patient; or, as the law finally read, when "in personal attendance" on his patient.

As the Act became uniformly administered by the Treasury Department, many leaders, like James H. Beal who had originally facilitated the bill's success through a system of triplicate order blanks, in the middle 1920s, raised serious doubts as to the intent of narcotic control at the federal level.

The Relationship between Business and Government

The relationship between business enterprise and government in the Progressive Era could be characterized as a partnership of economic nationalism or mercantilism.[99] In a mercantile society, government makes laws that favor or encourage business in an effort to control, but not own, the means of production. As the New Deal approached (whose ideas arguably gestated in the collapse of Progressivism after World War I),[100] government began to distance itself from business by instituting programs aimed at social welfare at the expense of industry. As Jackson noted,[101] "If private enterprise was to be allowed the power of self government under a relaxation of the antitrust laws then it owed something in return." New Dealers, like Assistant Secretary of Agriculture Rexford Tugwell,[102] certainly desired government to be the "dominant partner" in the partnership.[103]

The 1920s alliance of government and business culminated in the Market Crash of 1929 and the ensuing Depression.

Government's role was shifting from concern about the average citizen to the protection of both producers and consumers from each other and from natural uncertainty. The proper function of industry in the New Nationalism was to provide for the material welfare of the nation, not solely for pecuniary interests of business.[104] In the New Deal, government assumed a dominant role in recreating the economy by establishing production and price quotas, hiring labor, and distributing an expanding base of federal tax revenues to state-managed industrial projects.[105]

Federal commercial legislation clearly benefited large-scale pharmaceutical manufacturing over individual shop compounding during the 1920s and early 1930s, leading many consumer and professional groups to question the monopoly power bestowed on industry by government.[106] By the beginning of the 1920s, the federal government had developed the Department of Agriculture into the model scientific bureau of the executive branch.

During ethyl alcohol prohibition (1920-1933), no federal legislation was enacted to control medical or non-medical drug use to any significant degree. Organized pharmacy and medicine were engaged in continuous, often tempestuous, internal negotiations over materia medica[107] while industry was creating and patenting an entire array of synthetic pharmaceuticals.[108] Moreover, with the exceptions of Harvey Wiley, Martin I. Wilbert, and Lyman Kebler in the early years of regulation, government officials (heretofore distant from professional standard-setting organizations like USPC) became pivotal players who set standards for products in common use such as digitalis, ergot, and epinephrin.[109] By the early 1930s, the FDA retreated from this activity.[110]

Prior to the Eighteenth Amendment, taxes on the distribution of medicinal alcohol forced many pharmacists to sell beverage alcohol to pay for licensing fees. As Higby noted:[111]

> Not only did these [federal excise alcohol] taxes force pharmacists to use more factory-made drugs, but they also influenced other aspects of their practice. Because they had to obtain liquor licenses to carry medicinal alcohol, many pharmacists stocked beverage alcohol to pay for the license.

Moreover, these fees also drove industrial production of fluidextracts, a major dosage form innovation by Proctor used at the time.[112] Higby observed that individual pharmacists were financially unable to buy the huge quantities of alcohol needed to produce 1:1 formulations prescribed in the legally binding USP.[113] (These formulas were later negotiated to 10 percent.)[114] After the amendment, physicians wrote many liquor prescriptions, and pharmacies became one of the only sources of medicinal and beverage ethanol.[115]

The Perceived Need for an Arbiter

Why did the United States need an arbiter of pharmaceutical fact and whose interests did it serve? Why did the perceived need and government as a solution arise at that particular time in history? How else might it have played out? What if the USP and NF were not written into law as official drug standards? Mass production and the profit motive are often blamed for creating the inherent need for government intervention in many aspects of social intercourse during the period.[116] The fact that any market evolved with power concentrated in the hands of those who knew how to produce and controlled price is often referred to as "destructive competition."[117] What is apparent is that through sustainable bureaucratic structures, government harnessed the productivity of industry for the purpose of national welfare by the threat or actual use of physical force through seizure of property. Pure food and drug regulations were promulgated to solve the widespread public health problems of drug adulteration and misbranding by nostrum makers so that individuals could make better economic choices.[118] During the period between 1906 and 1938, scientific discoveries were providing necessary evidence in an evolving structure of scientific bureaucracy that would lay the foundation for effective state problem solving. To quote Dupree:[119]

> In the first ten years of the twentieth century, a government without science was already unthinkable. Excepting military applications, the government's scientific establishment was virtually complete in 1916.

The results of experimentation in medicine, driven by the understanding of specific causes leading to specific effects, were appealing to those interested in establishing a social structure that would protect, unify, and further the interests of the state for the protecting of citizens from commercial fraud and physical harm. Again, Dupree noted regarding the problem-solving methodology adopted by the federal government by the time of the New Deal:[120]

> Beginning in the 1880s, the bureaus [of Chemistry and Soils] had pioneered in developing the problem approach and had organized themselves around it. Having proved its

practicality, the problem approach now raised the question whether or not it was too practical.

Cultural tensions between various groups on several different levels were manifested in an evolving polity[121] structured by pharmaceutical fact. The occupational tensions between pharmacists and physicians regarding scope of practice played out in local practice as well as USP's Committee of Revision. As Jackson noted:[122]

> Each industry received significant concessions. The greatest trade victories, in FDA's view, came in 1935 and after. Notable among these were the more lenient regulations on label information, reduction in the power of multiple seizures, investment of advertising controls in the Federal Trade Commission, and the addition of elaborate court review provisions.

Market tensions between patent medicine producers, ethical pharmaceutical makers, and compounding pharmacists escalated to new heights as parallel therapeutic channels became competing alternatives for access to drug therapy. Simmons illustrated the prevailing professional attitude:[123]

> For many years the separation of the legitimate chemical and pharmaceutical preparations from those which we call choose to call secret nostrums has been a difficult task for those conducting medical journals, whose advertising pages it was desired to keep free from unethical advertisements.... The suggestion finally was made to broaden the scope of the proposed board by making its functions similar to those of the Committee on Revision of United States Pharmacopoeia; in other words, to have it take up the work where that committee leaves off, and to publish in book form a list descriptive of the preparations which conform to the required standard, but which are not official.

The constitutional tensions between the judicial, legislative, and executive branches of government at the individual state and federal levels became evident as first the judiciary (through decisions of courts), [124] then the executive branch (through notices of judgment)[125] dominated the role of arbitrating legislative will and intent. There were jurisdictional tensions regarding the scope and harmonization of law between the state and federal governments, and their relationships to and impact on local economies and individual citizens.[126] Challenges to the constitutional authority to direct federal intervention in individual's lives, as well as the constitutionality of United States Pharmacopoeia and National Formulary standards encoded in a federal statute came as a result of changes in the idea of sovereignty in a segmented society.[127] Even within the executive branch, the conflict over advertising (a form of speech) between FDA and the Federal Trade Commission led to delays in reforms of the 1906 law.[128] Family tensions between men and women with regard to work and home, and care of the infirmed also entered into the social negotiation through temperance movements and consumer activism.[129]

These tensions related to the uncertainties of changing social structures. The changes were brought on by collective identification, organization, and action, the rise of problem-solving bureaucratic management in government, the application of cause-and-effect scientific knowledge for commercial gain, the physical separation of the locus of production and consumption, and the movement of sick care from the home and family to institutions and medical professionals. Federal bureaus serving public, collective interests were replacing an engrained pluralistic system of patronage politics serving private, individual interests.[130] At the same time, corporate philanthropy heavily influenced the preservation of a corporate social structure designed to benefit production. Quoting Dupree:[131]

> Deepening the shadow cast over government by the universities was the dramatic rise of the foundations of men wealthy enough to rival the government itself...Carnegie Institution of Washington.... The General Education Board's [of the Rockefeller Foundation] early support of Seaman A. Kanpp's agricultural extension program actually led to a new function for the Department of Agriculture. The Rockefeller Foundation took the discoveries concerning hookworm and yellow fever, both developed within the government, not only into the Southern United States but to other parts of the world.

After the Spanish American war, American government had its first opportunity to demonstrate the effect of the scientific approach to medicine in the control of disease and illnesses such as narcotic addiction. Intervention by government in controlling the opium trade in the Philippine islands,[132] and in controlling cholera and malaria in Cuba, were the first attempts to establish and perfect the bureaucracies necessary to address health problems, as well as the application of police power for policy enforcement. Again, Dupree noted:[133]

> The emergence of the United States as a world power opened new horizons for the Army Medical Corps, which in defiance of all the rules had been readying its research tools for just such an opportunity. Sternberg, Walter Reed, and Leonard Wood had served for years at frontier posts in the West. When the focus of the nation shifted overseas, they and their colleagues went to Havana, Puerto Rico, and Panama. Their success reflected the long preparation sculptured by the Army Medical School, the Museum, and the Library.

Humphreys detailed the evolving federal authority after successful eradication campaigns by Gorgas in Havana.[134] The islands' populations were captive, had no agency or rights, and thus, were ideal populations for social experimentation.

Several historians have pointed out that these interdictions and interventions could not have happened in America at the time. Watts noted how the spread and control of Yellow Fever in the South was tied to racist ideas about blacks in the Mississippi Valley.[135] In a sense, American government at the federal level experimented overseas with the exercise of police power to control individual behavior unrelated to crimes against person or property. This should not be seen as simply colonialism or imperialism, the subjugation of the vanquished. The United States was establishing itself as a world power, and the executive branch was responsible for executing treaties.[136] Thus, on conquered soil, the federal government was "perfecting" the very bureaucratic mechanisms it would use on its own civilian population, to enforce domestic drug control, both medically and criminally.

Armed with the knowledge derived from occupation of the Philippine islands and Cuba, those government operatives then transplanted control mechanisms to America, and began to advocate, within the limits of the Constitution, for the use of physical force to achieve the government's disease and drug control policies. Initially, the use of physical force was limited to the act of seizure of property.[137] In other words, interdiction efforts were designed to take substances considered unfit for individual possession and consumption, and place those substances under a federal control mechanism designed to assure appropriate medical use.

Why were narcotics seen to be a threat to national sovereignty? A loose narcotic policy diminished America's emerging world role.[138] Did habituation pose a real threat to the nation's health and welfare? It supposedly lowered productivity, a major concern of corporate philanthropies like the Rockefeller Foundation.[139] What were the arguments for and against individual choice vs. state control of narcotic production, distribution, and use? Why were narcotics the first drugs to receive federal interest? Why not a uniform law on poisons?[140] (Regulated by the Hygienic Laboratory and its successors until 1972, biologics were not considered drugs at the time.)[141]

Certainly the state had an interest and claimed constitutional legitimacy for taxation in the commerce clause. It levied tariffs on many substances to raise revenue before income taxes, and opium use was quite common in the American population. Musto showed that per capita narcotic consumption, primarily opium, peaked in 1896.[142] He also argues that opium use was quite widespread in China at the time, and did not pose significant social problems to the Chinese people, only to government.

Moreover, Chinese populations that migrated to America were known to smoke opium for relaxation or for physical endurance. In addition, opium use, and its soporific effects, disengaged the desire to fight, making conquest of the population much more easily achieved. So, while Musto makes the argument that there really was not a problem with opium used in the Chinese civilian population, the British military understood the use of opium for trade and social control and for victory.

The Polity and Rationality of Government Intervention

The study focuses on the time between 1906 and 1938 because many scholars have determined that this was when federal government became directly involved in aspects of drug therapy.[143] This was during a time when the ideas of scientific investigation were receiving widespread application in military and civilian life.[144]

Several precedents indicated federal interest in certain aspects of pharmaceutical use.[145] Since the beginning of the Republic, the federal government had been interested in the health of merchant seamen located at ports on the American Coast, and started the Marine Hospital in New York. In 1813, the Vaccine Act was established in order to provide a pure and unadulterated form of smallpox vaccine. It was repealed in 1822. At the behest of medical and pharmacy practitioners, the Drug Importation Act of 1848 attempted to prohibit the trade of drugs between America and other countries that were adulterated or infested. This interest stemmed from the importation of infested and adulterated cinchona bark used to treat soldiers who were fighting in the Mexican-American war. Historians consider the Act a failure because of the mechanisms of patronage politics in the appointment of inspectors at each port along the Atlantic coast, as well as the lack of standards for identity and purity other than crude organoleptic methods.

By and large from the country's founding until the early twentieth century, the federal government played little role in the regulation of pharmaceuticals.[146] When it did, the focus of control was border management issues regarding foreign trade.

The federal government became interested in the purity of drug products only when it became scientifically possible to validate a substance's active constituents or proximate principles. These analytical techniques have their roots in the Department of Agriculture's Bureau of Chemistry, although investigations by physicians and pharmacists (notably Procter, Squibb, Bache, Wood, and Maisch)[147] constituted the basis for rational governmental intervention.

After the Civil War, the Department of Agriculture emerged as the first broad federal bureau that established a civil service component.[148] Under the direction Harvey W. Wiley, an Indiana physician who trained in Germany in connection with the Imperial Board of Health during the formative years of German unification,[149] the Bureau of Chemistry broadened its organic act and engaged in analytical testing for a wide variety of substances. The Post Office frequently consulted the Bureau in connection with patent medicine mail fraud.[150]

Publicly, Wiley was convinced that American businessmen were intentionally adulterating food products and medicines without telling the purchaser. Privately, he sought ways to induce a standard of value that would extinguish the commercial concerns of medicine manufacturers.[151] His group was mostly concerned with labeling fraud. To Wiley, it was dishonest to claim "cure" when the idea of curative properties for any pharmaceutical agent could not be scientifically demonstrated or validated at the time.

The broad social question at the time seems to have been, what institutional configuration would direct the social life of the nation?[152] Would it be through public administration and government bureaus? Or would entrepreneurial direction and market forces continue to predominate? Alternatively, would it be a mixture of government and market?

One way to examine this question would be to construct a grid with two axes that denote these two forms of social order. On the x-axis, the range of sentiment for market-based control, pro or anti, could be constructed. Pro- or anti-government sentiment as the basis of social control could be plotted on the y-axis.

The grid (see Figure 1.2) is made up of four quadrants that illustrate major social and political movements operative at the time in the United States. Those in the anti-market/anti-government quadrant, I will label anarchists. The anarchists advocated for no overarching social structure, other than that deriving from social exchanges between private individuals. Capitalists make up the pro-market/anti-government quadrant. They advocated for the strict separation of government and the market with private ownership and control of the means of production, and limited government's role to the protection of private property.

Figure 1.2
Social Order of Pharmaceutical Fact
PRO GOVERNMENT

"Socialists" "Democrats"	"Nationalists" "Progressives"
ANTI MARKET	**PRO MARKET**
"Populists" "Anarchists"	"Republicans" "Capitalists"

ANTI GOVERNMENT

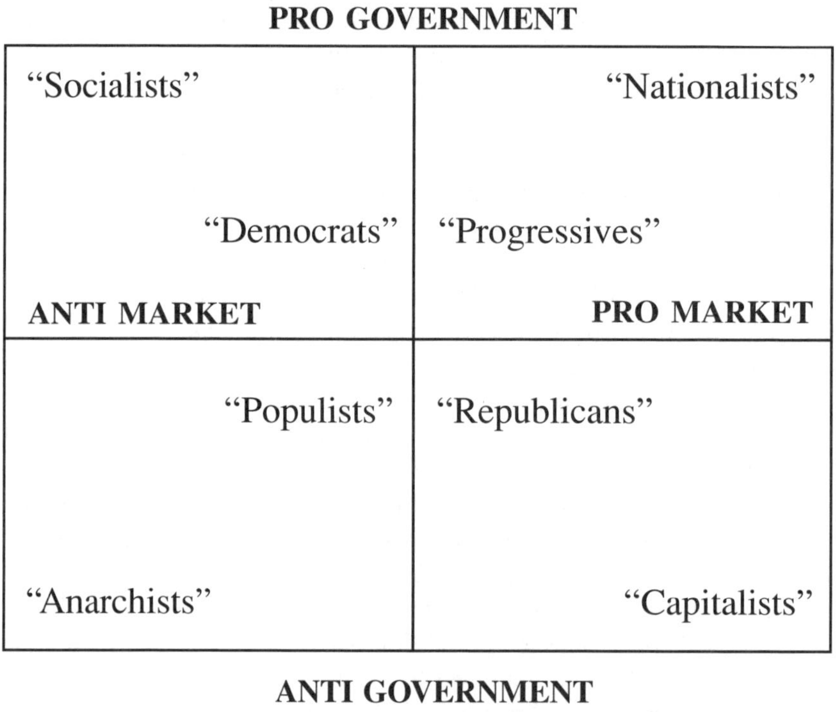

The Socialists can be found in the pro-government/anti-market quadrant. Socialists argued for government control and ownership of the means of production and distribution of wealth. The pro-government/pro-market quadrant contains the Nationalists. Nationalists advocated a social structure based on private ownership but government control of the means of production.

Near the center of the grid, predominant political parties can be found. For example, Republicans were less pro-market and anti-government than the capitalists. The Democrats were less pro-government and anti-market than the Socialists. The Populists were less anti-market and anti-government than the anarchists. Finally, the Progressives were less pro-government and pro-market than the Nationalists.

This grid is a visual synopsis of prevailing thought toward social organization. Through this polity (or social structure), legislation and regulation aimed at drug therapy control maneuvered through local, state, and federal jurisdictions.

The Interplay of Virtue and Vice

One can hear in the correspondence, arguments, and polemic a certain sense of social order resonating from each of these philosophies. The century began with the assassination of President William McKinley; a mercantile-oriented president financed by private "trusts" who led the country "out" of the "gay nineties." Leon Czolgosz, an anarchist, shot McKinley. When Populism turned into Progressivism as a result of the rising social solidarity of disenfranchised farmers, laborers, and women,[153] new visions of a symbiosis of business and government fueled a wide range of early social welfare activities. Narcotic and drug control were among these efforts, not only to provide the average citizen with pure pharmaceuticals for self-medication, but to stamp out vice and corruption.

Although from different origins, the complex interplay of vice and virtue was a common theme of social life in the Progressive Era that continued through the New Deal. Much depended on what was considered "narcotic." Virtuous pharmaceuticals for the average citizen, those that were ethical, were constituted from nature in indigenous form without any taint of vice due to narcotics or alcohol, without any synthetic processes that adulterated natural constitution.

As Progressivism waned in the realities of world war, ethanol prohibition was ratified in three-fourths of the states. The American Social Hygiene Association, a multidisciplinary group sponsored by the Rockefeller Foundation, sought to keep progressive social virtues in the public eye, and joined with the AMA in its sustained effort to rid the country of health quackery, especially regarding venereal diseases. A renewed sense of national conservatism, however, muted the government's role and support of a social welfare agenda, leading to an increasing array of business subsidies and favors.

With the Market Crash, government began a major effort to restructure the national economy. As he had as secretary of commerce under Harding and Coolidge, President Hoover directed the continuation and expansion of state controls in capital markets with the net result of rampant inflation in the early 1930s. In pharmacy, the idea of price maintenance (uniform prices for prescriptions) became incorporated into the National Recovery Act (NRA) as a result of the Cost of Medical Care survey conducted by then APhA president Robert Fischelis in 1932. Competition over prescription prices (an internal pharmacy concern since prices were not advertised to the public) was claimed to lead many pharmacists to sell other merchandise to remain viable. Repeal of the NRA stimulated retail pharmacy interests like the National Association of Retail Druggists to urge the passage of the Robinson-Patman Act that prohibited differential pricing from manufacturers to retailers. With the emergence of the chain pharmacy, employed pharmacists in New York City became the first health occupation to unionize.

As the transformation of pharmacy from its medical roots to a legal structure continued, the idea of a pharmaceutical became tied to a stock commodity instead of a therapy. This dichotomy, product versus people, was (and continues to be) unique to Pharmacy, and the dichotomy of ideologies in terms of commercial vs. professional was magnified. At the time, however, to Pharmacy, "people" was considered as "public," not as patients. Most pharmacists were concerned with making a living from medicine sales to the public not from judging the therapies of physicians, nor from ministering to unique pharmaceutical needs of individual patients. Throughout the period, the federal government needed some group that could set standards for both drugs as products of industrialization and as therapy. These questions would be left to the United States Pharmacopoeial Convention (USPC) and AMA's Council on Pharmacy and Chemistry (CPC).

Notes

1.   Young, 1974; Bakalar, 1984: 74.
2.   Jackson, 1970: 215.
3.   Marks, 1997: 41.
4.   Bakalar, 1984: 69.
5.   Ibid., 1984: 94-95.
6.   For explanation of the British context and an alternative viewpoint regarding the adequacy of the medical/legal dichotomy, see Berridge, 1990: 101-114.
7.   Dupree, 1957: 256-301.
8.   Young, 1967:41.
9.   Liebenau, 1981.
10.   Young, 1967: 64; Glover, 1920: 17-19.
11.   Brandt, 1987.
12.   Brown, 1979: 193-4.
13.   Okun, 1986: 288-9; see Porter, 1997: 628-667, on the relationship between medicine and society through the state.
14.   Morgan, 1981: 100; Musto 1987: 2.
15.   Simmons, 1905: 718-721; Sletten, 1959: 9.
16.   Morgan, 1981: 97.
17.   Parascandola, 1992.
18.   Marks, 1997: 21.

19. Hofstadter, 1955; Young, 1967: 66 details 1872 statute giving Postmaster General power to unilaterally declare mail fraud. For consumer activism, see Kallet and Schlink, 1933: 195-267.
20. Young, 1967: 53.
21. Link, 1954; Wiebe, 1967.
22. Brandt, 1987; Musto, 1987: 5.
23. Wiebe, 1962 and 1975.
24. Marks, 1997.
25. Simmons, 1905: 718.
26. Young, 1961: 205-225.
27. Brandt, 1987.
28. Morgan, 1981: 76-78.
29. Wiebe, 1962.
30. Kremers, 1940: 78. Pages 73-79 contain dates for state laws and associations.
31. Marks, 1997: 23-6.
32. Sonnedecker, 1982: 28-39.
33. Sonnedecker, 1986.
34. Higby, 1992: 53.
35. Risse, 1997: 51-73; Morgan, 1981: 104.
36. Higby, 1992: 63.
37. Young, 1970: 147-57.
38. Marks, 1997: 19.
39. Pure Food and Drugs Act of 1906 refers to those eleven drugs that are required on the label as "dangerous drugs."
40. Marks, 1997: 37.
41. Swann, 1988: 3; also Parascandola 1992.
42. Marks, 1997: 22.
43. Founded in 1907, the National Association of Boards of Pharmacy initially was concerned with development and harmonization of law as it related to pharmacist migration from state to state.
44. Formed in 1900, the American Association of Colleges of Pharmacy developed from the Faculties of Pharmacy group within the American Pharmaceutical Association, and today works closely with NABP to address educational and licensure issues.
45. Sonnedecker, 1986.
46. Jackson, 1970: 216.
47. Marks, 1997: 40.
48. Anderson and Higby, 1995.
49. Ibid., 1995.
50. Sonnedecker, 1986.
51. Higby, 1992: 47.
52. Kremers, 1940: 73.
53. Young, 1967.
54. Kremers, 1940: 78.
55. Sonnedecker, 1986; Kremers, 1940: 78.
56. State laws accepted the standards of several domestic and foreign pharmacopoeias.
57. This group included Lyman Kebler, who was also a member of AMA's Council on Pharmacy and Chemistry, the Federal Specifications Board, and USP's Committee of Revision.
58. Anderson and Higby, 1995.
59. Formed to address infant foods and formula issues.
60. Simmons, 1905: 719, "Members of the original 1905 Council on Pharmacy and Chemistry include: Arthur R. Cushny, C. Lewis Diehl, C. S. N. Hallberg, Robert A.

Hatcher, Lyman F. Kebler, J. H. Long, Frederick G. Novy, William A. Puckner, Samuel P. Sadtler, Julius O. Schlotterbeck, Torald Sollman, Julius Stieglitz, Martin I. Wilbert, and H. W. Wiley."

61.   Stewart, 1901: 1177.
62.   Stewart's company was a non-profit, private share company incorporated in New Jersey.
63.   Higby, 1992: 20.
64.   See King, 1987. Lyman Kebler trained in pharmacy under Prescott at the University of Michigan, and later received an MD degree from George Washington University. Between his pharmacy and medical degrees, he worked in the laboratories of Smith Kline and French.
65.   Wiley, 1930.
66.   Dupree, 1957: 275.
67.   Young, 1961; Simmons, 1905.
68.   Higby, 1992: 25-31.
69.   Maisch, 1868 cited in King, 1987: 66-67.
70.   Higby, 1992: 13.
71.   Sletten, 1959: 456.
72.   Simmons, 1905: 721.
73.   Musto, 1987: 13.
74.   Ibid., 1987: 58.
75.   Morgan, 1981: 105.
76.   Francis Stewart's correspondence to Robert Fischelis regarding pharmacy's place relative to medicine, law, and theology is found in the Francis E. Stewart papers, Wisconsin Historical Society, Madison, Wisconsin.
77.   Higby, 1992: 14-15.
78.   Morgan, 1981: 66.
79.   Musto, 1987: 59.
80.   Morgan, 1981: 74; also see Young, 1967: 44.
81.   See Martin I. Wilbert's comments on self-medication in Public Health Reports.
82.   Parascandola, 1997: 77-91; Morgan 1981.
83.   Liebenau, 1981.
84.   Swann, 1988; also see Liebenau, 1981.
85.   Wiley, 1929: 160-3.
86.   Hofstadter, 1955.
87.   Musto, 1987: 14-15.
88.   Hofstadter, 1955.
89.   Wiley, 1930.
90.   Young, 1967 claims that his message was not about fear.
91.   Ibid.
92.   Through poison laws, and later medical practice and pharmacy acts
93.   Morgan, 1981.
94.   Young, 1961: 231.
95.   Ibid., 241.
96.   Link, 1954.
97.   Terry and Pellens, 1928: 5, 67-69, 89-90; also see Schmeckebier and Eble 1923: 47-48, 56-57, 116-117.
98.   Musto, 1987: 58.
99.   Link, 1954.
100.   Hofstadter, 1955.
101.   Jackson, 1970: 202.
102.   Young, 1967: 158-190.

103. Jackson, 1970: 202.
104. Link, 1954.
105. Hofstadter, 1955; Wiebe, 1962.
106. Kallet and Schlink, 1933: 195-267; Lamb, 1936.
107. Dupree, 1957; Anderson and Higby, 1995.
108. Liebenau, 1981.
109. Young, 1967: 59.
110. Jackson, 1970.
111. Higby, 1992: 51.
112. Ibid., 67.
113. Ibid.
114. Ibid.
115. Ibid.
116. Ibid.
117. Young, 1967.
118. Bakalar, 1984.
119. Dupree, 1957: 288.
120. Ibid., 352.
121. Higby, 1992: 46. For a polity-centered approach, see Skocpol, 1992.
122. Jackson, 1970: 206; also see Anderson and Higby, 1995.
123. Simmons, 1905: 718-719.
124. Gates, 1934.
125. Jackson, 1970.
126. Many states were going to enact their own revisions to the 1906 Act, something industry did not want. See Jackson, 1970.
127. Wiebe, 1975.
128. Young, 1967: 174-5.
129. Lamb, 1936; Brandt, 1987.
130. Skocpol, 1992.
131. Dupree, 1957: 297-8; also see Brown, 1979.
132. Morgan, 1981; Musto, 1987.
133. Dupree, 1957: 290.
134. Humphreys, 1992: 149-78.
135. Watts, 1997: 239-247.
136. Morgan, 1981; Musto, 1987.
137. Young, 1967.
138. Bakalar, 1984; Morgan, 1981; Musto, 1987.
139. Brown, 1979.
140. Wilbert and Motter, 1912.
141. Kondratas, 1982: 8-27.
142. Musto, 1987: 3.
143. Sonnedecker, 1986.
144. Dupree, 1957.
145. Sonnedecker, 1986.
146. Swann, 1994: 55-70.
147. Higby, 1992.
148. Dupree, 1957.
149. Wiley, 1929.
150. Young, 1961.
151. Young, 1961; Wiley, 1929.
152. Wiebe, 1967.
153. Hofstadter, 1955.

2

Pharmaceutical Fact

Chapter 1 introduced the historical cultural context and meaning of drug use in American society between Progressivism and the New Deal. In this chapter, the social negotiation of "pharmaceutical fact" is presented to conceptualize the meaning of drugs as a therapeutic modality.

A dichotomous worldview prevailed during the time period between Progressivism and the New Deal. Ideas of rational or empirical, good or evil, domestic or foreign, safe or dangerous had a pervasive influence on what was thought to be in the best interest of the nation. These ideologies guided the actions of many conscientious individuals who shaped the social order to express that interest. Inhabitants in the country were separated into a number of groups—citizen and alien; producer and consumer; patient and criminal. These groupings led to the suspension of limited, representative government at the national level.[1] Further, the separation of citizens into producers and consumers began the development of a national economy based on the best interests of the federal (then called national) government.[2] Through the Post Office and regulation of the trusts, the federal government first became involved in modulating group interests after the Civil War.

The setting of standards for pharmaceuticals was concerned with the factual information obtained about the physical products themselves. Further, the exchange and application of therapeutic agents to and by people provided a physiopathological context for determining the evolving concepts of safety and efficacy that manifested in individuals. Pharmaceutical fact, as a social construction, includes both the issues of pharmaceutical scope and rational therapeutics because, whether implicit in the cultural understanding of the time or explicit in statute, standards constituted the major device for negotiating in each area. Standards embodied the best collection of working knowledge about scope and therapeutics.

Physicians, pharmacists, and attorneys during this time were trying to come to grips with the practical treatment uncertainties associated with unstandardized "secret" formulas and preparations. In addition, the very ideas of "proof" and "validation" were changing from individual organoleptic or sense-driven to numeric experimental-driven methodologies. Further, the uncertainties generated from deciphering the sacred, true, and natural from the profane, false, and artificial, created tensions within the professional communities. These tensions manifested periodically, first in legislation, then administrative regulation, to clarify uncertainty.

The primary cultural and professional need was to rectify chaos and uncertainty. The unintended consequences of legislation, however genuinely concerned with human suffering, led to the formation of a social system for drug therapy based on the founding tenets of federalism that usurped the rights of individual citizens.

That government would tacitly permit or abrogate individual citizens' rights is not a new conception. Many constitutional originators were very concerned with a federal approach to governing, and drafted amendments to restrict federal power—the Bill of Rights. Throughout the nineteenth century, arguments were made to the Supreme Court regarding the role of the national government in jurisdictional issues in and between the states. The Court characteristically affirmed, in decision after decision, the right of a state to conduct its affairs within its own borders. At least in theory, the Bill of Rights also afforded federal protection to individual citizens from infringement by the states. (Whether by conquest or purchase, annexed territories and other jurisdictions became another matter.)

As the populations of many coastal states, such as New York, Massachusetts, and New Jersey, doubled as a result of immigration during 1880-1900, public health concerns associated with crowding and foodstuffs began to play a key role in the governing activities of local municipalities. As sanitation practices brought under control the outbreak of many infectious diseases, public health advocates continually negotiated with private physicians for treatment venues and patients. Many, like Francis Thurber in New York, believed that government offered the better solution to public health problems, echoing the humanitarian idea that it was immoral to profit from the misfortune and sickness of others. Local law enforcement became impossible because many officials were personally acquainted or in league with, or received bribes from the would-be compliant. Because, in practice, public health compliance was really voluntary (even though statutorily required), many advocates became convinced that private practitioners would not change without draconian measures aimed at making them "toe the line."

Major coastal cities, especially New York City, Boston, and San Francisco, were key ports of entry for drug products from Europe and the Orient. Many counterfeit and adulterated substances were labeled as genuine articles. Many were not indigenous to the Continent, and lacked any method of organoleptic identification as genuine. As a therapeutic modality, drugs were not held to be curative for any ailment or disease. Most understood this, laymen and practitioner alike. Those that did not, and promised cures, were called quacks (from quack salving: quack derives from the application of salve to soothe or palliate). Drugs that were considered effective had to demonstrate a direct sensory causal connection to an ailment's mitigation.

Drug therapy that was considered substantial included those that affected the central nervous system, the skin, and the gastrointestinal tract. By substantial, I mean that the effects of drug therapy on these body systems were directly perceivable by patient and practitioner. Many states enacted poison laws as a part of their pharmacy laws modeled after American Pharmaceutical Association leaders John M. Maisch (1869) and James Hartley Beal later in the nineteenth century (1895). As measures to control fraud, these laws were largely ineffective because the local enforcement required to police commercial activity was considered secondary to criminal acts against persons and property. Even though improper dosing could lead to unintended toxicity, that arsenic use was pervasive, and that toxicological homicides may have been more common than realized, the federal government would not deal with issues of "poison" until much later.

In the introduction, I referred to one major purpose of this book— the exploration of how drugs and therapy were thought of by scientific, professional, and intellectual leaders between Progressivism and the "brain trust" of the New Deal. Pharmaceutical fact(s) is an idealized conception through which the negotiated physical constants and proximate principles of substances, as well as their therapeutic properties and uses, were transfigured into an independent-of-referent social system. By separating purported truth from purported falsehood—defining standards in terms of that which could be enforced by threat or actual physical force entrusted to government—the social system for drug therapy became a self-perpetuating mechanism through which therapeutic intervention could be applied legitimately to relieve human suffering by "duly authorized" practitioners.

Pharmacopoeial Scope

In the context of crude, unstandardized, and "secret" composition, pharmacists and physicians derived a somewhat meager living from practicing the craft of healing. Anderson and Higby noted:[3]

> The concept of "medical police" or "sanitary police" gained increasing acceptance in many states.... Grounded in the states' implied police powers, the medical police concept gave state governments considerable latitude in protecting the public health and served as ideological justification for organizing state boards of health, licensing health care professionals, and passing pure food and drug laws in state legislatures.

Often indistinguishable, practices by both groups in the nineteenth century consisted of the application of remedies only after the laymen's unsuccessful efforts to resolve their medically related problems. Both physicians and pharmacists alike listened to complaints, formulated impressions, and applied remedies that typically they personally prepared or oversaw. Some remedies worked; some did not. Practitioners were often convinced that if their recommendations did not relieve the situation, it was because of the wide variation in the characteristics of the available raw ingredients. Moreover, people often sought out other types of practitioners simultaneously to the extent of their economic means. Wide variation existed from practitioner to practitioner, from prescription to prescription, and from batch to batch.

To provide a better sense of clarify and uniformity (and reduce variation and uncertainty) at the practice level regarding pharmaceutical therapies, physicians and pharmacists in Philadelphia and New York City organized separately at mid-century to address domestic and international issues of drug integrity. Patterned after the fledging United States Pharmacopoeial Convention[4] the American Medical Association (AMA) and the American Pharmaceutical Association (APhA) began to negotiate with each other and government. To quote Anderson and Higby:[5]

> The Convention of 1890 decided that the term official would replace officinal in all pharmacopoeial publications. By 1890, state laws had made USP standards legally enforceable.... Begun as a book to bring uniformity to the communication between physicians and pharmacists, the USP had started taking on a broad regulatory role.

Initially, the negotiations consisted of naming and constituent functions (identity), methods of assurance (identification and purification), methods of production (standardized patient-specific and bulk compounding), and methods of application (therapeutics). Each of these functions was a source of evolving tension because there was no clear method for resolving conflict and differences of opinion. But, to William Proctor after returning from his only European visit, having agreed-upon sub-standard standards was better than having no standards at all. Moreover, the identity and purification of only a handful of alkaloids were known, and most identification, production, and therapeutic questions were addressed through the sense perception of the individual practitioner. How a substance looked, smelled, felt, and tasted—"organoleptic methods"—were all that could guide determination. Anderson and Higby commented:[6]

> Early in the revision process, many pharmacists complained that they faced prosecution under state laws for selling articles for commercial use that did not conform to USP standards. Some Committee members urged the adoption of two names in such cases, one for medicinal use and one for commercial use.

Later, as advanced methodologies and instrumentation provided additional information about constituents, controversy continued to exist over the properties of purity (solubility, melting point, natural adulteration, specific gravity, qualitative testing, and optical crystallography), nomenclature (common, Latin, commercial, and scientific), as well as questions of therapeutic and economic value related to posology (dosing and application) and nosology (classification of diseases).

Anderson and Higby found:[7]

> One focus of controversy between physicians and pharmacists was the status of proprietary drugs...trademarked products of an emerging ethical drug industry and promoted, in accordance with AMA requirements [from the Council on Pharmacy and Chemistry], chiefly to physicians.

In the view of many government officials, like AMA council members Harvey W. Wiley (a physician-attorney) and Martin I. Wilbert (a hospital pharmacist), laymen of the time were in no position to judge the validity of claims made by practitioners or makers of the patent medicines. Pharmacy leaders complained that AMA Council members desired that all drug use go through physicians. As Anderson and Higby pointed out:[8]

> [*National Druggist* editor Henry] Strong's principal theme was that AMA's purpose in attacking patent medicines was not solely, or perhaps even primarily, "to punish fraud"

but "to put a stop to all self-medication" and thus to attack a traditional cornerstone of the pharmacist's professional jurisdiction and livelihood.

"Professionals" believed that citizens could not reliably treat themselves. However, "businessmen and retailers" relied on self-treatment as a major source of their income. With no apparent and reliable referents for definitive standards, the American Pharmaceutical Association (APhA), the American Medical Association (AMA), and the United States Pharmacopoeial Convention (USPC) continually polled member practitioners for a majority opinion as to the veracity of proposed position statements on individual composition and standards for drugs and therapy. According to Anderson and Higby:

> The [USPC]Committee continued the policy of lowering standards when necessary in the interest of enforcement, while the Department of Agriculture's problems in implementing the Food and Drugs Act allowed the committee some breathing room in its work.[9]

Further, they noted that a key point of departure and separation between physicians and pharmacists was the issue of pharmacopoeial scope.[10]

> The early 20th-century frictions between physicians and pharmacists crystallized around the issue of pharmacopoeial scope—that is, what would and would not be included in the USP. In general, physicians saw the USP as a select compendium of the best and most useful therapeutic agents, holding to its original vision of an instrument for imposing a measure of uniformity and consistency on therapeutic decision-making. Physicians, then, attached paramount importance to the Committee of Revision's drug selection mission, aimed at keeping the USP abreast of the latest trends in drug therapy. Pharmacists, meanwhile, tended to see the USP as a modern compendium of drug standards, adapting the latest science and technology to the making of drug standards but remaining widely inclusive in scope and leaving questions of drug selection and therapeutic efficacy in the hands of medical practitioners.

All professional groups were convinced that ordinary, untrained people could determine neither what constituted a pure drug nor its proper application. James Hartley Beal, a pharmacist-attorney and Dean of Pharmacy at Scio College in Ohio, was instrumental in guiding the language of the Pure Food and Drugs Act of 1906 (1906 Act). Again, Anderson and Higby:[11]

> James Beal was a prominent member of that congress [Food and Drug Congress] who served on a special committee that claimed responsibility for writing much of the final bill [of 1906]. In fact, Beal claimed personal responsibility for the section of the Food and Drugs Act dealing specifically with the USP.

The evolution of standards in the United States Pharmacopoeia (USP) and the National Formulary (NF) up to the turn of the twentieth century was considered sufficient enough to a majority of professionals (many who had never practiced their profession) to rationalize enforcement by government. The USP included a standard for alcohol that led to controversy because "rectifiers" violated in the official manufacturing process by adding alcohol to their products. Anderson and Higby wrote that "alcohol was a second prickly scope issue during the ninth revision...whiskey was defined in USP VIII."[12]

Conflict continued between the professionals, but a compromise on therapeutics and necessities was reached, as Anderson and Higby noted:[13]

> A gentleman's agreement at the Convention's 1920 meeting...pledged to honor its physician members' authority to decide on admission of "therapeutically active substances" to USP X while reserving questions involving "pharmaceutical necessities" to pharmacists.... The search for a compromise...did carry organizational dividends, ensuring the continued collaboration of medicine and pharmacy in the making of the USP and restoring USP's image.

Enforcement of these standards would result in protection of both producers and consumers. However, to be effective, enforcement would also separate citizens into mutually exclusive producer and consumer groups. Both government and a maturing synthetic pharmaceutical industry weighed in to influence pharmacopoeial standard-setting. Anderson and Higby commented:[14]

> The admission of proprietary products to the USP was symptomatic of a closer working relationship between the USP and the pharmaceutical industry at a time when the industry was enhancing its reliance on and investment in scientific research.... Work on the 10th revision during the 1920s also highlighted a closer working relationship between the Committee of Revision and government agencies...the Bureau of Chemistry agreed to provide packaged, standardized product samples—the first "reference standards"—for industry use in complying with several of the bioassay methods mandated in USP X.

In the beginnings of this system, a consumer of drug therapy could not be a producer because law would provide this basic form of self-protection. Moreover, producers would be required to define their goods in terms of a label, and the contents could not vary "in any particular" unless stated on the label. Those particular substances specified on the label were so designated because, in the therapeutic and criminal context of the time, their status as therapeutic interventions was not questionable to laymen or practitioners. These pharmaceuticals worked, their identities and purity could be defined and assured, and the consequences of overuse were manifested everywhere in society (in the sanitarium, in opium dens, in saloons, in homes, and at work). "The question of standards soon became a major stumbling block."[15]

How and why these substances, as well as others, worked therapeutically and pharmacologically were key questions to an evolving science of what, in 1902, Francis E. Stewart called "pharmacotherapy," the uniting concept between pharmacy and medicine. Nevertheless, both food and drug producers united behind the 1906 Act because these regulated industries perceived great benefits from uniform legislation. To quote Anderson and Higby:[16]

> A dramatic change in industry attitudes toward regulation was a major factor in passage of the Food and Drugs Act, with the giants of the food industry in particular endorsing federal regulation as a means to rationalize newly emerging national and international markets.

Rational Therapeutics

Stewart's idea of standards for pharmaco-therapy was tempered in the fires of Hell's Kitchen as he practiced medicine and treated "poor blood" by inventing "desiccated, defibrinated, bullock's (ox) blood" injections. His activities caught the attention of George Simmons, editor of the *Journal of the American Medical Association*. On reading Stewart's paper on the formation of a "National Bureau of Materia Medica," Simmons published a modified version in the journal. Stewart's approach, a non-profit shareholder corporation, was somewhat contrary to the editor's stance. Standards for physical products and their application would be ensured by professionals, not enforced by government. Alternatively, the British-born Simmons was of the opinion that government should be intimately involved in professional standards-setting activities. Leaving it to professionals had failed in Britain between 1859 and 1876. Looking to propel AMA into national prominence and solve the quackery issue scientifically and politically, he enlisted key leaders from medicine, pharmacy, and government to create the Council on Pharmacy and Chemistry. The Council was charged with the responsibility of establishing an endowed "therapeutic reform to the public to combat the nostrum evil within its own ranks."[17] His editorial on the difference between secret nostrums and "ethical" proprietary products laid out the ground rules for the Council's pronouncements on pharmaceutical preparations.

Not only did economical self-directed remediation by citizenry need encoding in an evolving national statute. Professional-directed therapy needed a reliable and valid methodology for making scientifically sound recommendations. The Council generated a set of ten rules that guided their decisions on therapeutic worth. Council decisions were published in *The Propaganda for Reform*. Because the USP and the National Formulary did not address commercially available preparations, the Council subjected each substance and nostrum to intense scrutiny related to identity, nomenclature, marketing, availability and access, and therapeutic claims. The Council Rules became the therapeutic road map for rational scientific practice in drug therapy.

Rule 1 specified that "no article (The term "article" shall mean any drug, chemical, or preparation used in the treatment of disease.) will be admitted unless its active medicinal ingredients and the amounts of such ingredients in a given quantity of the article, be furnished for publication. (Sufficient information should be supplied to permit the council to verify the statements made regarding the article, and to determine its status from time to time.)"

Under *Rule 2*, "no chemical compound will be admitted unless information be furnished regarding tests for identity, purity and strength, and, if a synthetic compound, the rational formula."

Rule 3 prohibited admission that included public advertisement. "No article that is advertised to the public will be admitted; but this rule will not apply to disinfectants, cosmetics, foods and mineral waters, except when advertised in objectionable manner."

What became the most contentious, therapeutic claims without informed, educated opinion were disallowed in *Rule 4*. "No article will be admitted whose label, package or circular accompanying the package contains the names of diseases, in the treatment of which the article is indicated. The therapeutic indications, properties and doses may be stated. (This rule does not apply to vaccines or antitoxins nor to advertising in medical journals, nor to literature distributed solely to physicians.)"

The labeling and description of appropriate candidates needed to contain the actual source and derivation of raw materials. *Rule 5* stated that "no article will be admitted or retained about which the manufacturer, or his agents, make false or misleading statements regarding the country of origin, raw material from which made, method of collection or preparation."

Cases where manufacturers obviously misstated a product's worth were dealt with in *Rule 6*. "No article will be admitted or retained about the therapeutic value the manufacturer, or his agents, make unwarranted, exaggerated or misleading statements."

To further clarify *Rule 2* in reference to toxic or dangerous substances, *Rule 7* provided that "labels on articles containing "heroic" or "poisonous" substances should show the amounts of each of such ingredients in a given quantity on the product."

Many nostrums were named with catchy, memorable trademarks that stimulated often ill-advised purchase and use. According to *Rule 8*, "every article should have a name or title indicative of its chemical composition or pharmaceutic character, in addition to its trade name, when such trade name is not sufficiently descriptive."

In *Rule 9*, the Council required information about the property status of products with copyrights and registration information the manufacturer supplied to government. "If the name of an article is registered, or the label copyrighted, the date of registration should be furnished to the council."

Finally, *Rule 10* mandated the disclosure of a discoverable patent to the Council. "If the article is patented—either process or product—the number and date of such patent or patents should be furnished. If patented in other countries, the name of each country in which the patent is held should be supplied, together with the name under which the article is their registered."

While *"Rule 4* contains the most explanation and comments on the rules which the committee referred to as radical," it served as the basis for the greatest number of rejections for approval as a new and non-official remedy. And, in addition to the physician and manufacturing pharmacists and chemists, they also pertained to the retail druggist in commercial trade.

Experience has clearly shown, however, that it is not safe to enumerate on the package the diseases of which in article may be indicated, since this is also the means by which the laity, *who are not competent to determine whether or not its employment is safe and proper*, may be induced to continue its use or to recommend it to others quite regardless of the evident dangers of forming drug habits or of doing serious injury *by employing a remedy that in reality may be contraindicated*. It is the *physicians' prerogative* to determine in what disease the article may be indicated, and he is *not* supposed to go to *the drugstore* for his knowledge regarding this. It is not the function of the pharmacist to recommend or to prescribe medicines but only to be familiar with their pharmaceutical and chemical characters, strength and dosage and with the best forms of administration.... It is asserted that the naming of diseases on the label of the package is necessary, because many physicians will be unable to tell from the therapeutic properties alone in what diseases and medicinal article may be indicated. This may be true with a certain class of doctors, but it isn't certainly not true with the best majority of the educated, progressive physicians of America, and this is the class whose interests are concerned in this movement.... The council, however, is unanimous of the opinion that this method of exploiting the medical profession is one of the principal causes which made the best physicians hesitant to prescribe any proprietary medicines, have led others into irrational therapeutics, have made pharmaceutical tyros believe that they could prescribe just as well as the physicians, and have been the means the causing scores of these medicines to be used for self medication by the laity, to the detriment and sometimes to the serious and permanent injury of the person taking them. (*Original emphasis*)

It is clear from these Rules of the Council that consumers' self-directed care with patent medicines was considered a social evil, one that could be minimized through professional oversight by these academic physiologist-pharmacologists and pharmaceutical chemists (practitioners of medicine and pharmacy were not represented at all on the Council). Moreover, there were no consumers on the Council, and no rules to help individual citizens make reasonable, informed choices about therapeutic selection. The central idea was to make therapeutics a rationalized endeavor based on the evolving tenets of experimental science as opposed to empirical observation and its attendant *post hoc, ergo prompter hoc* fallacy. Consumers had to seek informed professional counsel in order to be assured of the facts about pharmaceutical therapy.

Pharmaceutical Fact as a "Modern Fact"

Pharmaceutical fact can be thought of as an idealized, drug therapy-related version of what Poovey called "the modern fact." The central thesis of her argument on the changing nature of factual veracity in the modern world was that proof and validation began to be derived from numerical representations detached from their descriptive sensory perceptual data. Moreover, numerical conclusions, at first derived from enumeration and later association, became ascendant; numbers served the rationalized purposes of the modern state. The state could and did use numerical facts to apportion representation, collect taxes on production and consumption, and distribute the spoils of political processes.

Poovey noted: [18]

On the one hand, because Western philosophy since the seventeenth century has insisted that the things we observe constitute legitimate objects of philosophical and practical knowledge, many people think of facts as particulars, isolated from their contexts and immune from the assumptions (or biases) implied by words like "theory," "hypothesis," and "conjecture".... On the other hand, because philosophers have always sought to produce systematic knowledge, which has general, if not universal, application, some people think of facts as evidence that has been gathered in the light of—and thus in some sense for—a theory or hypothesis.... At the very least, what counts as a fact can never escape the idea that the knowledge that matters is systematic, not simply a catalog of observed but unrelated particulars.

Why Poovey selected the sciences of wealth and society was deliberate and fascinating in light of the estimation by physical scientists of the utter subjectivity of human social endeavors. Moreover, that cultural trading and social interaction required numerical abstraction is not lost on Poovey. Only until better statistical measures based on a more tenable mathematical conception (discovered by an English agrarian-priest named Fisher interested in raising agricultural production) could physical science purport the causal associations of unobservable phenomena. Poovey goes on:[19]

> [The] focus on the sciences of wealth and society [is] because…among the first to rely on numerical representation as a critical component of knowledge production…the collection of numerical information helped consolidate government power in England in the thirteenth and fourteenth centuries…and this process resumed at the end of the eighteenth century.

Where did this system of numerical representation derive? Poovey pointed to accountancy, a fact confirmed by Weatherford regarding the de Medici family: [20] The first English double-entry manual in…1588…[was] rough translation of an Italian text published in 1494.

Again, quoting Poovey:[21]

> [Bacon's] famous aphorism "knowledge is power" should be taken in this context [of reorienting and strengthening the Tudor monarchy]: as a statement about the instrumental value that a certain kind of knowledge could have for a specific form of political power.

Pharmaceutical fact comprised of these two branches—pharmacopoeial scope and rational therapeutics—is a variety of the modern fact in several ways. First, prior to the establishment of standards, the identity, identification, and estimation of purity of crude substances were governed by the perceptual abilities of individual pharmacists, physicians, and laymen. These organoleptic methods were described in the United States Dispensary, the United States Pharmacopoeia, the National Formulary, and other foreign pharmacopoeias and recipe books. Although considered the basis of law enforcement in various states, a plethora of "standards" repositories, notwithstanding word-of-mouth formulas passed among the generations, lacked the metrics of rationalized, scientific proof. Often tried as a yardstick, description was not an effective and consistent state defense for property seizure, personal detention, and/or assignment of punitive damages. Charges based on description were dismissed. Verdicts were often overturned on appeal.

Secondly, the national government became interested in enforcement of professional standards as a statutory issue only when it was possible to determine, in numerical terms, the active constituents of any substance as a matter of experimental scientific fact. Based primarily on its border-policing powers, the federal government's first two entries into control of drug products came at the behest of pharmacists and physicians in New York who were eager to supplant the "secret," unstandardized nostrum trade with a professionalized rubric of its own making.

Each law failed to protect citizens, in part, because inspectors could not systematically determine identity or purity, even by reference to professional associations of pharmacists and physicians organized at the time for that very purpose. Administratively, inspecting substances became a political patronage position at many ports across the eastern seaboard. While claims of foreign dumping and adulteration were rampant especially at the time of the German Revolution in 1848, there was no hard-and-fast way to judge natural from intentional from artificial adulteration.

Lastly, only a numerical standard divorced from the perceptual description of actual substances could become the foundation for professionally directed therapeutics. What was considered therapeutic was a learned matter. Drug use considered non-therapeutic was labeled criminal, because self-treatment was, at root, a capricious vice, left to the vicissitudes and proclivities of human nature. The average citizen was not morally or intellectually competent to make the choices that directed his/her own life. Left alone, citizens would make the wrong choices that would be harmful to the state's interest.

Employment of Means for the Attainment of Ends

Having addressed pharmaceutical fact as a guiding social force in the evolution of standards and as a modern fact (meaning enforceable by the state), I now analyze another component, that of goal-directed action. According to Misesian praxeology:

> The result sought by action is called its end, goal, or aim. Strictly speaking the end, goal, or aim of any action is always the relief from a felt uneasiness. A means is what serves to the attainment of any end, goal, or aim.... Goods, commodities, and wealth and all the other notions of conduct are not elements of nature; they are elements of human meaning and conduct. [22]

Whether related to medical remediation, general economic exchanges, or national legislative policies, all human conduct is undertaken by individuals to change their present, less desirable state of being to a future, more desirable state. Mises realized[23] that, even in the context of medical practices of the time, whatever laymen and practitioners considered "factual" directed action by both parties.

> Present-day medicine [in the 1930s] considered the doctrine of the therapeutic effects of mandrake as a fable. But as long as people took this fable as truth, mandrake was an economic good and prices were paid for its acquisition.

As long as the results of using mandrake were thought to be ameliorative, despite professional opinion, people exchanged what they possessed for the narcotic and emetic properties of the "nightshade" alkaloids it contained. From the user's perspective, the uneasiness may have been pain. The means may have been chickens or cloth or money that was offered in trade. Or, the user may have foraged the surrounding woodlands for an indigenous source of supply if she knew what mandrake looked like. Practitioners of medicine and pharmacy may have discounted the therapeutic value of mandrake, offering in its place opium, belladonna, or henbane. Nevertheless, to the person in pain, the end, goal, or aim was relief of the condition. The practitioner or producer of mandrake may have provided alternatives to mandrake, or, wanting to satisfy the user, may have prepared and sold what they considered a less effective, but desired medicament to the user in pain. From the user's view, the only expectation from using mandrake or any other alternative was to be relieved from the sensation of pain. The practitioner had to decide whether the user's expectation could be met within the extent of their knowledge, skill, and substances at their disposal. The "standard" for both user and practitioner was whether mandrake (or opium, belladonna, or henbane) was valuable enough to exchange for pain relief in that individual user. Mises continued:[24]

> The ultimate ends of human action are not open to examination from any absolute standard.... They apply to the means only one yardstick, viz., whether or not they are suitable to attain the ends at which the acting individuals aim.

In this example, pain decreases anyone's functional abilities that may or may not indicate a latent physiopathological process. Pain may inhibit the ability to work and make a living, care for one's family, and maintain social relations, either temporarily or permanently. Again, quoting Mises: "The immense majority of men [and women] aim first of all at an improvement of the material conditions of well-being."[25]

No action can be taken with absolute certainty of result, not in medical treatment or any other circumstance. There are no guarantees that a particular course of action will cause a given and desired result. Likewise, there are no standards that can substitute for guarantees, except that an individual can decide to pursue or change a chosen course by his or her own standard. Mises pointed out: [26]

> The uncertainty of the future is already implied in the very notion of action. That man acts and that the future is uncertain are by no means two independent matters. They are only two different modes of establishing one thing.

The actions available to both users and practitioners within the therapeutic context of evolving legislation and regulation became restricted to behavior that was judged as moral, efficient, and rational. Those normal and professional actions considered profane, wasteful, and irrational became criminal and subject to prosecution by an evolving federal apparatus. About action—whether initiated by individual or collective—Mises noted: [27]

> Every action is always based on a definitive idea about causal relations.... It is the individual who thinks.

What became manifested in American culture at the turn of the twentieth century was the idea of professionally directed standards for drugs, foods, and other basic commodities in common exchange. Because consumers could no longer be treated rationally as producers, and because both groups (producers and consumers) may make choices in conflict with state or national priorities, let alone their lives or those of their families or neighbors, standards of behavior and substance in the exchange of goods and services would drive the modern national government. After all, who could be against "standards" for pure food, pure drugs, and pure production by qualified producers?

In the context of material gain and medical treatment, only those uninitiated in the laws of scientific inquiry could hold as a standard of value their own benefit. What professionals of the time did not consider was the social impact of their standards on the livelihoods of others they purported to serve. To conclude with Mises:[28]

> For all parties committed to pursuit of the people's earthly welfare and thus approving social cooperation, questions of social organization and the conduct of social action are not problems of ultimate principles and of world views, but ideological issues.

Scope and Therapeutics Constituted a Negotiated, Fact-Based Polity for Standards

Polity is normally thought of by social scientists, like Skocpol, as the institutional configuration of government and of political parties.[29] In this instance, the meaning of polity is much broader. The polity, or social structure, of standards setting was constituted in both government and professional organizations like the United States Pharmacopoeial Convention (USPC) Committee of Revision, AMA's Council on Pharmacy and Chemistry, and APhA's Committee on Unofficial Remedies and National Formulary Committee. Federal law was written in 1906 that vested political power in the standards of the USP and National Formulary.

Mises posited the idea that human social conduct, including action and cooperation, derives from an overall interpretation of life, what he called a worldview. However, what made that worldview real and actionable for individuals was an ideology. It is through an actual interpretation of all the events in an individual's life held in that context that the idea of worldview could function effectively in guiding action. As Mises pointed out, a worldview, by itself, does not suffice: All individuals act in the world, not in their minds.

> A world view is, as a theory, an interpretation of all things, and as a precept for action, an opinion concerning the best means for removing uneasiness as much as possible. A world view is thus, on the one hand, an explanation of all phenomena and, on the other hand, a technology…. The concept of an ideology is narrower than that of a world view…only human action and social cooperation…the totality of our doctrines concerning individual conduct and social relations.[30]

What Wiebe called "the search for order"—by producers and consumers, citizens and government alike—continued throughout the early twentieth century. Standards-setting activities were, at first, entrusted to professionals by government. As professional standards continued to fall short of enforcement, officials in the Department of Agriculture, especially the chemists and pharmacologists, began to question the reliability and validity of the rubrics of medicine and pharmacy. The rubrics were not sufficient in the detail required for the federal government to exercise police power, to seize property, to apprehend and prosecute offenders, or to render justice.

Beginning in 1933, Rexford Tugwell led the executive charge to remedy the failings of the Pure Food and Drugs Act of 1906. Government, not voluntary professional associations and corporations, would become the arbiter of pharmaceutical fact regarding scope and therapeutics. Many professional leaders who encountered direct experience of the social maladaptation codified in the 1906 Act echoed the sentiment.

However genuinely concerned with human misery and economic fraud, "producers" convinced government that "consumers" needed them to continue to create standards. To government, standards for drugs and their therapeutic application came to be thought of as guarantees of integrity and propriety. Substances became legislated and codified into federal existence, and defined in terms of enforcement.

The 1906 Act seemed to be a commonsense approach to food purity. From these simple beginnings, a complex social system evolved where all stakeholders (except citizen-patient end-users) lobbied for their version of the sacred, true, and natural. All other contrary behavior and action was, by definition, criminal. The processes of alcohol and narcotic use initially generated revenue for the national government (contributing to the elimination of the tariff system). However, use of these substances not directed by medical and pharmacy professionals from an enforceable legal code for some therapeutic end of the practitioner's choice became illegal. The consumer had only one choice to make: be a patient or be a "bootlegger."

Harvey Wiley knew very well, in 1912, that enforcement of the 1906 Act was indeed a tall order in federal court. The federal government could not enforce standards written as "rubric." (In the context of pharmaceutical fact, and to professionals of the time, "rubric" was the descriptive directions for identifying and preparing drug products.) So convinced that businessmen were intentionally and wantonly adulterating commercial substances of all kinds, like whiskey, Wiley led the pharmacopoeial charge to define the proper medical use of spirits containing ethanol.

According to the 1910 USP, whiskey was meconium derived from a four-year, fermentation process of grain extraction aged in oak barrels. Nothing else could be traded or consumed as whiskey. No combination of artificial colors, flavors, water, or distilled ethanol could be added to or substituted for mash. Wiley even questioned the propriety of using any alcohol in medical practice.

While James Hartley Beal publicly always gave credit to Harvey Wiley, privately he took pride in realizing the inefficiency of government-directed codification of standards, and the achievement of official investiture of pharmacy-controlled standards. Very active in the drive for enactment of the 1906 Act, American medical leaders were left out of the initial transfiguration of standards to statute brought about by USP and NF. An ensuing thirty-year battle with organized pharmacy would begin to dominate interprofessional discussion, often leading to deeper separations over pharmaceutical scope and rational therapeutics.

Notes

1. The Native American population had been decimated. Interestingly enough, Article XVII of the Bill of Rights authorizing the direct election of United States Senators was ratified on 16 May 1912. Article XIX of the U.S. Constitution on women's suffrage was ratified on 26 August 1920. These two events were the final triumph of a social process begun by the Anti-Saloon League, a mixed gender group whose activities led to replacement of the saloon as the venue for male-only political conventions.
2. Post Office Regulation 17 Stat 322-23; Interstate Commerce Act of 1887; Sherman Act of 1890.
3. Anderson and Higby, 1995: 216; for the origins and meaning of the medical police idea; and for general discussions of late nineteenth-century state regulatory intervention, they cited Rosen, 1953: 21-41; Brock, 1984; and Campbell, 1980.
4. Anderson and Higby, 1995: 181.
5. Ibid., 180.
6. Ibid., 210.
7. Ibid., 224.
8. Anderson and Higby, 1995: 225-6; they cited Strong, 1912:333.
9. Anderson and Higby, 1995: 221.
10. Ibid., 207.
11. Ibid., 218.
12. Ibid., 227.
13. Ibid., 207-8
14. Ibid., 232-3.
15. Ibid., 228.
16. Anderson and Higby, 1995: 217. For a description of how the food (and drug) industries induced favorable legislation, see Barkan, 1985:18-26.
17. Simmons, 1905: 718-721. How these rules guided the federal approach to drug regulation and other issues are discussed in Marks, 1987 and 1997.
18. Poovey, 1998: 1.
19. Ibid., 4.
20. Ibid., 3.
21. Ibid., 98.
22. Mises, 1949: 92.
23. Ibid., 93.
24. Ibid., 95.
25. Ibid., 96.
26. Ibid., 105.
27. Ibid., 177.
28. Ibid., 181.
29. Skocpol, 1992: 41; also Skocpol, 1995: 103-6.
30. Mises, 1949: 178.

3

Letters between Leaders

This chapter examines the correspondence between James Beal and Edward Kremers in order to better understand the cultural tensions present within American pharmacy from early Progressivism to the New Deal.

Why Beal and Kremers?

Professor Beal and Dr. Kremers (as they referred to each other in correspondence) had a lively interaction, from 1895 to 1939, about pharmacy's cultural, political, and professional positions.[1] They came from different personal backgrounds and political affiliations, and provided different kinds of leadership as pharmacists' educational and political thought evolved. But, both helped to transform pharmacy from a commerce-based, unregulated trade to a science-based, law-governed profession.

James Hartley Beal (1861-1945) and Edward Kremers (1865-1941) both grew up in the clannish society of independent families that characterized American culture after the Civil War. His kin on the Continent before the American Revolution, Beal was raised in rural Ohio along the Tuscarawas River valley.[2] After his family immigrated to America during the German Revolution of 1848, Kremers grew up in urban Milwaukee under the influence of the German Reform movement.[3] They were born and died within five years of each other. They corresponded with each other throughout their adult lives, and were business associates in the Midland Publishing Company located in Columbus, Ohio. Each founded, edited, and published pharmacy journals. Each started, directed, and taught at schools of phar-

---

Based on a presentation to the American Institute of the History of Pharmacy, American Pharmaceutical Association 148th annual meeting in Washington, DC, 17 March 2000.

macy and dentistry (Beal), and pharmacy and chemistry (Kremers). Each testified before the federal government in various venues on a variety of pharmaceutical subjects. Both men were Remington Medallists in recognition of their intellectual leadership within the profession.[4]

With prior training as an attorney in the common law tradition at the Cincinnati College of Law, Beal tended to address statute formation and commercial issues. As a phytochemist with German scientific education at Göttingen, Kremers gravitated toward the scientific basis of pharmacy practice. Beal approached codification of practice from the legal side of science: Kremers approached it from the scientific side of law. Their dialogue transpired in the middle. Correspondence began over the issue of educational standards for pharmaceutically related schools. It seemed to end in disagreement over government-initiated modifications to the federal Pure Food and Drugs Act of 1906, the proposed Tugwell Bill.

The Cultural Context between Progressivism and the New Deal

At the turn of the twentieth century, any American adult could buy any medicinal product made by any manufacturer for any purpose from any party of his or her choosing.[5] Forty years later, a system of social controls had developed to govern the identity, purity, labeling, manufacturing, safety, and access of pharmaceutical therapy. While most pharmacy organizations had stemmed from the American Pharmaceutical Association (APhA), a primary conflict arose between the more scientific, public-health-minded groups and the more commercially oriented groups.[6] Through efforts of the American Medical Association (AMA) Council on Pharmacy and Chemistry, academic medicine endorsed an evolving set of standards that became the basis for federal drug regulation in the 1930s and 1940s.[7]

In the twentieth century, society moved toward more formal, legal regulation in the control of drugs.[8] Self-medication was an established cultural process of drug therapy in the United States. Between Progressivism and the New Deal, two distinct, mutually exclusive categories at the federal level pertaining to drug use had developed—medical and criminal.[9] In addition, the drug control system became established to address economic and social welfare inequities that resulted from evolving divisions of labor in the professions and industrial society. Both in size and budgets, corporations rivaled government to influence the social life of the nation. During this period, the federal bureau system became firmly established in the executive branch, especially in the departments of Agriculture, Commerce and Labor, and Treasury.[10] As a result of the Pure Food and Drugs Act of 1906—the so-called "Wiley Act"—the United States Pharmacopoeia (USP) and the National Formulary (NF) became official standards of drug integrity. After the "Wiley Act," while description on the label of a substance was often tried in court,[11] the identity, purity, and uniform potency of medicinal agents was negotiated by pharmacy-trained individuals in many groups organized for that specific purpose.

Pharmacy associations, interprofessional groups like the United States Pharmacopoeial Convention (USPC) Committee on Revision[12] and the American Public Health Association's Committee on Food and Drugs,[13] intraprofessional groups such as the National Drug Trade Conference (NDTC),[14] the Committee on Unofficial Standards of APhA[15] and AMA's Council on Pharmacy and Chemistry, and private non-profit corporate groups such as Francis Stewart's National Bureau of Materia Medica[16] and National Bureau of Medicines and Food[17] all addressed drug constituent and therapeutic questions from their particular viewpoint. AMA's *New and Nonofficial Remedies* provided practicing physicians with a listing of useful, unlisted, non-proprietary preparations. The *United States Dispensary*, originated by physicians Wood and Bache of Philadelphia,[18] provided another commentary on drug standards for practitioners of both disciplines[19] as well as Edward Kremers' *National Standard Dispensary*.

The Department of Agriculture's Bureau of Chemistry established a Division of Drugs under the direction of pharmacist-physician Lyman Kebler in 1907. In 1923, the Federal Specifications Board was developed with leadership from the National Bureau of Standards (1901) and the Association of Official Agricultural Chemists (1884).[20] The Association of Official Agricultural Chemists was formed to facilitate communication between state chemists with leadership from Bureau of Chemistry Chief Chemist Harvey W. Wiley (a former Indiana state chemist). Many members of these professional groups were trained both in pharmacy and medicine, and held appointments and leadership positions simultaneously in multiple groups.

The cacophony emanating from private professional efforts to create enforceable standards also resonated in the evolving structure of the federal bureau system, heard especially in the Departments of Agriculture and Treasury. As reflected in correspondence between Beal and Kremers, legal statute-formation at all levels of government was one major instrument of social structure for pharmacy. Administrative regulations were an unintended consequence of law. Legislative intervention by professionals became an institutionalized process of government sponsorship for the sanctioned uses for drug therapy. Acting on the precedents following enforcement of the Sherman Act, the Bureau of Trade and, later, the Federal Trade Commission of the Department of Commerce, began to codify "classes of trade."[21]

Major credit for drug therapy legislation has been given to Hamilton Wright, Harvey W. Wiley, and Rexford G. Tugwell; they were functionaries of government. However, as a private citizen, James Hartley Beal was intimately involved in the legal processes leading to statutory control of drug standards, alcohol, and narcotics. Beal attended every meeting of the National Pure Food and Drug Congress. His "unofficial" activities led others to codify the USP and NF into the 1906 Act. Eleven, mostly "narcotic," drugs were mentioned specifically in the 1906 Act because of both their social and scientific status in Progressive America.[22] Beal's "official" activities as organizer and chair of the National Drug Trade Conference (NDTC) helped achieve foreign policy—a "workable" domestic narcotic law.[23] Beal's suggestions also created the possibility for compromise of the Tugwell and Copeland Bills and reform to the 1906 Act, the 1938 Federal Food, Drug, and Cosmetic Act. Beal had become American pharmacy's statesman. Kremers was its scientist-reformer.

The Educational Reform Years—1895 to 1910

Beal first wrote to Kremers in 1895 to enlist Kremers' support for an organization of faculties of pharmacy.[24] Beal was unsatisfied with efforts by the American Pharmaceutical Association membership to find common ground for education standards between "old line colleges" and the new publicly funded, university-based schools. "Old line colleges" were those that were established by local pharmacist organizations, the first was the Philadelphia College of Pharmacy (1821). Beal's school, nestled in his boyhood surroundings in Harrison County, Ohio, was neither old line or publicly funded. Beal asked Kremers four questions: (1) Do you favor a separate organization? (2) Will the University of Wisconsin support it? (3) What school membership credentials would be required? and (4) What are the important issues in your opinion? Beal maintained that there was "still plenty of common ground" for educational reform.

Kremers did not reply to this initial inquiry, prompting Beal to write that he had correspondence from prominent schools of the United States, but not from Wisconsin.

> As yet have not been favored with your reply...I have replies from nearly all of the leading schools of the United States...university schools are favorable to the plan, while many of the old line colleges are not, preferring to take their chances with the American Pharmaceutical Association.[25]

Beal offered a mail order pharmacy program through the *Pharmaceutical Era* (called the "Standard Institute of Pharmacy") in conjunction with the school (PhG diploma) he started at Scio College in Ohio.[26] Succeeding noted chemist F. B. Power, Kremers was the second director of the course in pharmacy at one of America's premier land grant universities, the University of Wisconsin at Madison. Under his leadership, Wisconsin was the first school of pharmacy in the United States to offer a Bachelor of Science degree and the Ph.D. in the pharmaceutical sciences. He was the editor of the *National Standard Dispensary*, a compendium of scientific methods for pharmaceutical preparations and practical formulae. In 1902, as president-elect of APhA, Beal was an elected member of the Ohio General Assembly from the Harrison-Carroll district. Kremers was president of ACPF.[27] Both were members of the Executive Committee of the American Conference of Pharmaceutical Faculties (ACPF) that later became AACP.

Beal's course in pharmacy through the mail perhaps raised Kremers' suspicions as to Beal's intentions. The *Pharmaceutical Era* offered correspondence "finishing" for pharmacists at the turn of the century, one of many such proprietary educational endeavors that, to Kremers, may have typified substandard scientific education in pharmacy. The *Era* also offered financial incentives to students enrolled in colleges and schools, and was distributed every Thursday for a subscription of $1 per year. On letterhead stationery from the *Pharmaceutical Era*, Beal remarked about whether Kremers would be supporting a joint "scholarship program in the Department of Pharmacy at the University of Wisconsin" [28] and the *Era* course.

Kremers either did not answer or did not keep his answer to Beal's letters. In a 1902 letter, Beal provided a biographical sketch at

Kremers' request.[29] He knew of Beal's activities in the National Food and Drug Congress, in APhA's Section on Education and Legislation, and through mutual friends like George Beecher Kauffman of Ohio State University and Julius Koch of the University of Pittsburgh. Since Beal was elected president of APhA in 1902, Kremers may have wanted a record for historical purposes. Beal wrote, "in compliance with your kind request, I am sending you herewith a biographical sketch." The sketch indicated Beal's educational pedigree, association activities, and business interests in "manufacturing, banking, water works construction and operation, etc." While not specifying that his pharmacy degree was honorary, he noted his pharmaceutical graduate degree from the Ohio Medical College (now The Ohio State University College of Medicine) in 1894, and his election "to Ohio legislature from the Carroll-Harrison District, November 1901."[30]

In his brief legislative service, Beal was the author of the Ohio Municipal Option Bill (allowing townships to vote on the legality of ethanol beverage sales) as well as Ohio's Poison Law. A cartoon in the May 21, 1903 *Bowerston Weekly Patriot*, a local newspaper from Beal's district, depicts the local interrelationships between the saloon and the pharmacy.[31] Beal was perceived by the press to desire ethanol laws that would stimulate sales at pharmacies. Success in these two events had a tremendous impact on Beal's approach to future legislative review and promulgation for pharmacy practice.

Beal concluded from an ACPF meeting with Kauffman and Koch in Madison, "we had a great time in the woods, and returned home feeling that Wisconsin is the only state in the Union worth living in."[32] Beal had high regard for the educational and research abilities of Kremers, as well as his vision for education.

On further reflection, Beal commented that "the period at which a young man should get his preliminary training is at the time when he is most anxious to get into business, and he is likely to avail himself, therefore, of any excuse that will lessen the time which he must put in the high school or in the college of pharmacy."[33] Nevertheless, he believed "that we are making substantial progress, and that it is not going to take us as long as it took the medical profession to reach a satisfactory standard of preliminary requirements."

This may have been a reflection of Beal's own feeling as a teenage horticultural entrepreneur gathering medicinal plants in the woods along the Tuscarawas River for local pharmacists. He never practiced pharmacy as an adult after leaving the pharmacy of Warner and Hollander to pursue a bachelor's degree in pharmacy at the University of Michigan with physician-chemist Albert B. Prescott in 1880.[34] He did not finish his pharmacy degree, and returned to Scio to complete his Sc.D.

Kremers held the editorship of *Pharmaceutical Review* from 1896 to 1908, first as *Pharmazeutische Rundschau* (Pharmaceutical Review) with fellow German pharmacist Frederick Hoffman. A practice-oriented, scientific publication, *The Review* was purchased by the Midland Publishing Company in 1909 and merged into Beal's *Midland Druggist* to become the *Midland Druggist and Pharmaceutical Review*. The combined journal ceased publication in 1926.[35]

As expert in his own right in the stereochemistry of terpenes, Kremers replaced Harvey Wiley as the expert in volatile oils on the Committee of Revision of the USP in 1910. Wiley had assumed the presidency of the Convention. Beal became chairman of the Board of Trustees. In a letter to USP Chairman Joseph P. Remington, Kremers expressed concern over the voting methodology regarding identified inconsistencies.[36] This concern related to a troublesome movement among the states, highlighted in a previous Beal letter. The contention that standards established in statute could not be modified without new legislation signified "the uncertain standing of that provision of the Food and Drugs Act which seeks to make each revision of the Pharmacopoeia automatically displace the preceding one."

Kremers heavily endorsed Beal as Harvey W. Wiley's successor to be chief chemist of the Bureau of Chemistry.[37]

The Statesmanship Period—1910 to 1924

A member of the newly established USP Board of Trustees in 1900, Beal was elected chairman of the board in 1910. When the "saccharin issue" and "rectified whisky" sealed Wiley's fate as bureau chief, Beal was widely known to political leaders and academics alike. With its influence as one of the first colleges of pharmacy in the United States, the New York College of Pharmacy endorsed Beal as Wiley's successor at the Bureau of Chemistry. C. A. Mayo of the New York College of Pharmacy solicited support on Beal's behalf from three eminent pharmacy deans: George Beecher Kauffman of Ohio State, Julius Koch of Western College of Pharmacy in Pittsburgh, and Kremers. In a telegram to Kremers, Mayo announced,

"New York college of pharmacy last night endorsed Beal as Wiley's successor. Can you get endorsement of your and other universities? Have wired Kauffman and Koch." [38] Kremers contacted a Rochester, New York canner named R. A. Badger with close connections to Vice President James S. Sherman. As secretary of the Curtice Brothers Co. of Rochester, New York, preservers, Badger wrote to Sherman to support Beal's candidacy, referring to Beal as "John H. Beal, coming from Ohio, and being a Republican...a man fully capable..." [39] After sending his letter to the vice president, Badger wrote to Kremers, "I may be making a mistake in feeling, as I have, that manufacturing concerns, or those who have interests at stake, should not advocate the candidacy of any man." [40] Badger knew Kremers from Congressional testimony regarding the sodium benzoate content in canned vegetables and fruits. Prior to senatorial and vice-presidential offices, Sherman represented canning interests whose personal appeal to Theodore Roosevelt over the safety of saccharin, in Wiley's presence, led to the formation of the "Remsen Board" and Wiley's "retirement."

George Beecher Kauffman wrote to Kremers on 27 March 1912, alerting him to the grassroots movement for Beal's nomination, and urging him to communicate with the president of the United States. [41] In a letter to President William Howard Taft, Kremers detailed the nature of the person who should rightfully receive appointment as chief chemist.

> The administration of the law calls not only for courage of conviction and integrity, it also calls for common sense on the part of the person or persons who are called upon to administer it...who not only has the confidence of the sane public, but one who can be expected to take a broad view of the situation, one who will never sacrifice the best interests of the public but one who will not antagonize honest men who have an opinion different from his own by calling them liars, thieves, and murderers...if the country be the gainer, we [in pharmacy] sustained a loss for the greater good. [42]

Kremers received in return a standard letter from C. D. Hilles, secretary to President Taft regarding Beal's nomination. [43] To Kremers, James Beal certainly possessed these qualities of character: He formed his opinion about Beal and the predecessor, Harvey Wiley, firsthand, and, in his mind, there was no comparison. Harvey Wiley was a self-promoting politician; James Beal was a pharmaceutical statesman.

In the end, Columbia-trained physician Carl Alsberg, not Beal, was selected by President Taft to replace Harvey W. Wiley at the

Bureau of Chemistry. Beal did not initiate the drive for his nomination as chief chemist, and, throughout the appeal, continued to solicit Kremers' scientific expertise regarding a number of subjects, like Wilbert's "USPH Digest of Comments, [#79] from the scientific and teaching standpoint."[44] In his capacity as general secretary of APhA, Beal often called on Kremers to lend his scientific expertise to APhA. Lamenting on the tiring and complicated nature of association expense reimbursement, Beal remarked,

> Under our present system [of reimbursement and disbursement], bills, after being O.K.'d by those who present them, must go to the General Secretary, to the Finance Committee, back to the General Secretary, to the President, to the Treasurer, to the Chairman of the Council and back to the Treasurer; a complication which would not be tolerated for a week by a business organization.[45]

By 1914, Beal had relinquished his position as general secretary and editor of APhA's journal. Beal had periodic bouts with Bright's disease, a common kidney ailment of the time, perhaps brought on by his frequent use of acetanilide for pain relief. His son, George Denton Beal, assumed a professorship at the University of Illinois—Urbana. James Beal began a new position at Illinois' Urbana campus as director of Pharmaceutical Research, a position he held until retiring permanently to Fort Walton, Florida. Ever interested in indigenous plants as well as furthering his son's career, Beal made several inquiries regarding Kremers' scientific work in volatile oils.[46] Kremers replied that several presentations could be arranged based on current research from the country's first Pharmaceutical Experiment Station.[47]

> One on "Digitalis," a second "On the Alkaloidal Standard of certain drugs and their Fluid Extracts," and a third on "Tincture of Peppermint for Coloring Purposes."[48]

James Beal maintained his curiosity about "...advances at the first Pharmaceutical Experiment Station established in this country," wanting to pattern his own investigations at Illinois after the methods Kremers established at Wisconsin.[49] Kremers kept James Beal informed about the extent of "our Monarda [wild bergamot] work."[50]

George Denton Beal received Kremer's continued intellectual and research support because of his commitment to scientific progress in vegetable drug pharmacology. "I am trying to find a satisfactory drug mill for grinding root drugs...I am trying to establish the work in plant analysis here on a firm basis."[51] Kremers replied, "Dr. Newcomb of the University of Minnesota can, no doubt, tell you all about the mill [manufactured in Minneapolis] since he has one as part of his milling process."[52]

The campaign by AMA's Council on Pharmacy and Chemistry against the "secret" formulas of proprietary preparations prompted Beal to comment, in a 1917 letter, that physicians desired an unfair advantage in disclosing product constituents. "They want everybody else's formulas and prescriptions to be open, but insist upon the right to keep their own prescriptions secret."[53] Kremers saw another side of the issue. "As a matter of fact, I have been told that not a few of the flavoring extract manufacturers are extensive manufacturers of proprietary medicines."[54] James Beal was aware of their widespread penetration of the market, telling Kremers,

> I have known for some time that flavoring extract manufacturers have been handling a line of proprietary medicines, most of them of the variety sold through country merchants, such as diarrhoea and cholera balsams, liniments, cathartic pills, etc. Comparatively few of these preparations are advertised or are known to the regular drug trade.[55]

Both Beal and Kremers were anti-Prohibitionists but voiced disgust at the occurrence of pharmacy sales of beverage alcohol, common before and during Prohibition. Although not a "reformer by law," Beal argued for scientific practice codified in federal statute.[56] Kremers argued for scientifically dependent, cooperative manufacturing codified in state law.[57]

Beal and Kremers had extensive prior experience with sociocultural organizations bent on elimination of beverage ethanol. In his prior experience as an Ohio legislator, Beal had successfully crafted the Ohio Municipal Option Bill that allowed citizens to vote on the sale of ethanol-containing beverages in their locale. Kremers was very concerned about the impact of Prohibition on the pharmacist's ability to produce fluidextracts, a predominant dosage form of the early twentieth century. Later, in 1923, Beal argued to the Bureau of Internal Revenue for changes in the handling and taxation procedures for industrial grade alcohol.[58] There was also evidence available to both men that flavoring extract manufacturers were making and dealing in unlabeled, alcohol-containing proprietary medicines.

After the full effects of enforcement of the Harrison Anti-Narcotic Act (where thousands of physicians and pharmacists were prosecuted for "maintaining" all kinds of "habitués") and Prohibition, Beal found himself in a "foreign" country whose language he did not speak.[59] Kremers kept at his phytochemistry, formulating standards for volatile oils in the first Pharmaceutical Experiment Station in the United States while maintaining close contact with the LaFollette family's perennial campaign for presidential power.[60] With enactment of Prohibition and its impact on fluidextract and flavoring production, Beal related,

> I have personal knowledge of the fact that it is the intention of the heads of the Anti-Saloon League, if they can do so, to absolutely prevent the sale of any preparation containing alcohol which can, under any circumstances whatever, be used as a beverage.[61]

One of Beal's proposed remedies to pharmacy's lack of standing with government after World War I was to separate scientific research from the educational and legislative mission of the American Pharmaceutical Association. Beal advocated this separation as a way to pool resources independent of association politics. He also saw great advantages to the appointment of Kremers to its directorship. Organized like the "...National Research Council...the objects of pharmaceutical research could best be accomplished by a separate organization and an independent fund...a small Research Council of the A.Ph.A. which would name a Chairman or Director..."[62]

In a long response, Kremers echoed Beal's frustration with scientific progress for drug standards through professional committees:

> The sum total of the efforts of these committees, to my way of looking, has been that the hours spent on deliberations had better been spent on actual research.... The offer of the position of "Director of Research of the A.Ph.A. or of Federated American Pharmacy," might induce the University authorities to relieve me of some of my present routine duties.[63]

He then described his experience and the details of operating a university-based, multidisciplinary research organization, including financial arrangements for fellows and assistants, to bolster his candidacy. "We not infrequently get more help from the departments of Experimental Breeding, Plant Pathology, Entomology, and Horticulture than we do elsewhere." Kremers also indicated the disinterest of academic medicine in a program of systematic pharmacology:

> While we have a strong Department of Pharmacology in the School of Medicine, its professor and his staff are too much interested in problems of his own (oxidation in the animal body) to take a serious interest in our problems of systematic pharmacology as related to the study of vegetable drugs and synthetic new remedies.[64]

In the years following World War I, Beal and Kremers shared similar concerns about eroded relations between organized medicine and pharmacy. Beal wrote,

> My experience with the medical profession as regards the disposition to grant concessions to pharmacy has not been very favorable. I believe I told you of my experience

something over a year ago when a prominent MD told me frankly that they did not want pharmacists to have rank in the Army, regardless of their educational qualifications, since it would reduce the authority and influence of the medical officers to the extent that pharmacists were given recognition.[65]

Beal was a pharmacy consultant to the federal government during the First World War, and knew firsthand why pharmacy wasn't given the status afforded to medicine by government. (Many historians have attributed lack of status to lack of scientific pharmaceutical education at the time.)

One medical man with whom I talked told me that pharmacy would not be recognized, no matter what evidence was presented, since such recognition would mean that a corresponding amount of power would be taken from the medical authorities in the Government Service and this would not be permitted.[66]

Beal contended that individual pharmacists could not afford to manufacture because of increases in alcohol taxes by the federal government.

The proposed increase of the tax on non-beverage alcohol to $6.40 per proof gallon, with so-called draw-back privilege, will put the final quietus upon galenical manufacturing by the small dealer. The larger manufacturer can make use of the draw-back privilege. The small dealer cannot.[67]

According to Kremers, large commercial interests and the "drawback" privilege had created economic conditions within the practice that could not be reversed unless cooperative manufacturing could be established with intervention by government.[68]

The druggists, who have worshipped at the altar of commercialization, are themselves to blame, and I am awaiting with much interest the progress, positive or negative, that is being made in Europe as to the socialization of the apothecary shops.

Beal did not share Kremers' enthusiasm for cooperative manufacturing or his disdain for commercialization in the practice. Rather, the idea that the standards of a "tyrannical and fanatical minority who are, temporarily at least, in control of legislative activities in this country" was most troubling to Beal, a trend to which "…I am on principle opposed to further yielding."

I have always agreed with you in the proposition that pharmacists themselves have been chiefly to blame for the absorption of their functions by the manufacturing laboratories, and I also agree that it is hopeless to expect that the rank and file of pharmacy will ever make any earnest effort to recover their lost functions. There is a chance for developing a new race of pharmacists—small in number as compared to commercial druggists— who will from choice cultivate professional pharmacy.[69]

Kremers wrote a personal reflection about Beal for a future historical work after their visit in 1922. He summarized Beal's character as one who "has never been a reformer, least of all a reformer by legislation...[and] has never been a hustler, but rather a contemplator."[70]

> He [Beal] has always scorned the idea of improving mankind by laws. To him, laws are but the embodiment of the practices of mankind...[and according to] Dr. [M. G.] Motter..."Beal is lazy".... His "laziness" is that of the fisherman who enjoys fishing for the sake of fishing, rather than for the sake of the fish. It is the "laziness" of the camper who will stand mosquitoes, or an atmosphere of smoke in preference to mosquitoes; of the yachtsman who can spend five weeks on a cruise bringing his boat from one harbor to another, unirritated by storm that compells him to seek refuge in harbors for several days at a time; of the smoker, who truly enjoys his cigar, preferably while watching the glow of coal or wood in the fireplace, and who thinks his best thoughts while thus "employed".... Beal has never been a hustler, but rather a contemplator.

By this time, Beal had considerable influence within the United States Chamber of Commerce. Kremers could have perceived Beal as an operative of the National Association of Retail Druggists. In a letter to Secretary Henry, of NARD on 8 January 1923, Kremers asked,

> Are the retail pharmacists of this country of the eighty percent [of citizens], who are afraid to say "We are in favor of supporting the law, even the prohibition amendment, but we are going to insist on our constitutional rights as American citizens to have all laws, even the sacred constitution amended if we desire such amendment for the best of our country; and we shall brand as enemies of our country all those who in any way seek to curtail our rights as citizens of the United States?"[71]

Beal received a copy of Kremers' letter to Henry, and replied, "people are becoming very impatient with the intolerance of the minority that seems to be in control of our national policies." He believed that "when the right [national] leadership appears, I believe the people will be ready to follow it and overthrow the present autocracy."[72]

> My pet grievance is that the powers reserved to the people and to the States by the US Constitution have largely been stolen away from them, and that to-day our laws are dictated to a very great extent by small but highly organized and strongly financed minorities.[73]

The Conflict over Commercial Issues—1925 to 1939

Anna G. Bagley was James Beal's personal secretary, and former APhA auxiliary operative under Beal's administration. Now as the principal of the Midland Publishing Company, she announced a December 1924 stockholders' meeting.[74] The firm had been in a deplorable state since the death of George Beecher Kauffman in 1922, losing advertisers and subscribers alike. It had been sixteen years since the merger of Kremers' *Pharmaceutical Review* and Beal's *Midland Druggist*, and Kremers was ready to return his Midland stock certificates to Miss Bagley after several exchanges with Beal during 1925 and early 1926.[75] Kremers seemed to want to avoid any further commercial association with Midland. Finally, Beal wrote to Bagley, "Dr. Kremers has always acted very generously with respect to the Midland Publishing Corporation, and especially in this surrendering of his stock interest."[76] He informed Kremers that he had forwarded the stock certificates to Miss Bagley.[77]

On the issue of price maintenance, the two men were divided. Clear to both men, pharmacotherapy had become an economic and political component of the national economy. Regarding the Capper-Kelly Bill for price maintenance, Beal asserted that the interpretations of the Sherman Act had become a major legal way to restrict competitors' property rights. Kremers asked why not make a "real profession out of pharmacy" through science instead of through what he considered trivial issues like price maintenance. The real evils of commercialism would "not be wiped out, but they may be dealt with."[78] Beal believed that it was proper to base commerce on any producer's property rights so that an individual pharmacist could practice without becoming "criminal by merely doing what their large and successful competitors may do lawfully."[79] Kremers argued that, although not really important for professional pharmacy, commercial interests could be regulated for public welfare.

> When it comes to a consideration of price legislation as a whole, I still feel that if the time, effort, and money had been spent on improving the professional status of pharmacy, something really worthwhile might have been gained.[80]

Harvey Washington Wiley was somewhat of a nemesis to both Kremers and Beal, but for different reasons. To Kremers, Wiley "played" the role of scientist. Beal thought Wiley was politically naïve. Kremers had received a letter from Lyman Kebler that stimulated him to write to Beal about his memory of events in the movement for food and drug controls. Reflecting on Wiley's recent death and his books in 1930, Beal and Kremers helped each other place in context some of the events of their separate interactions with the chief chemist. Wiley had taken virtually all the credit for enactment of the 1906 Act. Wiley had castigated Kremers' 1902 testimony on sodium benzoate as a food additive in his 1929 book. About Wiley's book, *A Crime Against the Food Law*, Kremers wrote, "So far as my participation in that 'crime', it has been amply justified by legal action in almost all of the states of the Union."[81] Beal wrote,

> My recollection concerning the enactment of the Food and Drugs Act of 1906 is that many prominent pharmacists who were members of the A.Ph.A. were active in promoting that law. I believe I attended every meeting of the National food and Drug Congress, and did so at my own expense. Among the most active of the members of that organization I recall Remington, Chas. Caspari, Dr. Eccles, Seabury, N.O. Sanders, Chas. E. Dohme, Ebert, Hechler, and Hopp of Ohio, and myself. We did all that we could to formulate an effective measure and to secure its enactment by [the US] Congress.[82]

In the same letter, Beal indicated that he knew the process that propelled Wiley to the presidency of the USP Convention in 1910 at the same meeting where Beal was elected chairman of the Board of Trustees. It was an "unusually well organized and astutely conducted campaign" even if Wiley was unaware of it.[83]

Most of the correspondence after 1935 concerned the nature of their physical health and personal activities. One of Beal's last letters to Kremers detailed Beal's role in the evolution of the Pure Food and Drugs Act of 1906. Beal was not an official delegate to the 1898 National Pure Food and Drug Conference, but suggested that APhA leaders could promote a new bill based on regulation of interstate commerce. "The A.Ph.A. members whom I knew were almost unanimously in favor of it."[84]

At age seventy-three, Beal informed Kremers that he was traveling to Washington to work on a compromise measure to extract the worthwhile material contained in the Tugwell and Copeland bills. He wrote to Kremers after these negotiations in Washington, and strongly denied being a lobbyist for any organization. Of course, Beal was independently wealthy.

> I am not in the employ of the Proprietary Association of America or any manufacturer of proprietaries; neither have I accepted a retainer or the promise of a retainer from any pharmaceutical manufacturer or other person…. On several occasions while in Washington it was intimated to me that various associations would be glad to remunerate me for my services and expenses on account of the Tugwell Bill. To each of them I replied that I could not accept any such remuneration.[85]

What Would Make a Profession Out of Pharmacy?

Why did Beal and Kremers correspond over their entire adult lives?[86] It would be simple to say that both men believed pharmacy deserved professional status. Their written correspondence is replete with their solutions to pharmacy's problems of the day. There are several reasons, though, that may explain why they corresponded for almost fifty years.

Beal genuinely admired Kremers' pedagogical and scientific abilities. He expressed that sentiment repeatedly to Kremers. He may have sent his son, George, for Ph.D. studies at Columbia on Kremers' advice. First at the University of Illinois, and later at the Mellon Institute in Pittsburgh, George became an eminent pharmaceutical chemist, and set many production standards for industrial materials. In 1941, like Kremers and his father, George became a Remington Medallist of the American Pharmaceutical Association.

Kremers, on the other hand, seemed to appreciate Beal's political acumen and sense of controversy. He was working on his book on the history of American pharmacy, and knew that Beal was in the thick of every piece of federal legislation related in any way to pharmacy. Perhaps Kremers may have also wanted to influence Beal's legal pronouncements and negotiations.

The early years of their relationship were centered on educational standardization for pharmacy. They differed on the name of the pharmacy degree. Beal favored a professional three-year doctor of pharmacy (Pharm.D.) as one of the degrees he offered at Scio College because it conferred political and social status equivalent to the doctor of medicine (M.D.). Kremers developed an academic bachelor of science in pharmacy degree at Wisconsin in 1907. He advocated for the BS Pharm because its curriculum placed pharmacy on the same plane as other BS programs of the universities. Beal believed that the Pharm.D. (non-clinical) would bring political and commercial success for a new breed of practitioners. Kremers held that commercial and political worth would derive from an academic scientific education. Both men had little respect for practitioners and leaders of medicine. However, they had different reasons for this opinion our profession has yet to resolve: the commercial-scientific dichotomy.

Because Scio College was a private institution, Beal may have been concerned that it would not have the resources to offer the BS Pharm degree like the one at Wisconsin. He convinced the board of trustees to merge Scio's pharmacy program with Koch's Western College of Pharmacy (now the University of Pittsburgh) in 1908. Beal became an emeritus professor there, and a trustee of Mount Union College in Ohio when it absorbed the rest of Scio College. At the public university, Kremers persisted with the voluntary scientific degree. That degree became mandatory nationally for future phar-

macists by academic and licensing bodies in 1932. He went on to
establish M.S. and Ph.D. programs in the pharmaceutical sciences at
Wisconsin.

The statesmanship period (1910-1925) concerned each man's rise
to prominence. Beal was a moderate Republican and reluctant par-
ticipant in the evolution of every piece of federal legislation regarding drug therapy. An ardent Progressive Democrat, Kremers worked
to build a model of pharmacy education and practice in the state of
Wisconsin. However, both men put their affiliations aside in order to
elevate the status of pharmacy in government and in other professions. Despite these political differences, Kremers' in his network-
ing and letter of recommendation to President Taft showed his commitment to support Beal. Beal was pharmacy's consensus candidate
for chief chemist to replace a shared nemesis, Harvey W. Wiley. To
Kremers, Beal was worthy of the profession's and government's trust.
At the time he first wrote to Kremers, Beal had questioned the constitutional basis for national pharmacy, food, and drug laws.[87] Moreover, while the Beal-led National Drug Trade Conference had worked
out the professional practicalities of the Harrison Anti-Narcotic Act,
Kremers doubted whether narcotic law would be effective in controlling narcotic use.[88] Both men were against Prohibition because of personal tastes as well as Prohibition's impact on feasibility of a pharmacist to compound galenical preparations. Beal considered Kremers
the leading candidate for directorship of a proposed scientific research
organization separate from the American Pharmaceutical Association.
The Pharmaceutical Experiment Station proved that Kremers' idea of
attracting federal funding for research was correct. Beal emulated
Kremers' operations at the University of Illinois in Urbana.

During and beyond the 1890s, drug production became increasingly industrialized. Because of their different political and educational backgrounds, Beal and Kremers were sometimes in conflict
over the commercial aspects of personal and professional issues.
This conflict is epitomized in correspondence associated with the
demise of Midland Publishing.

Chairman of the USP board of Trustees until 1940, Beal had re-
tired from educational involvement. Kremers remained director of
the School of Pharmacy at Wisconsin until 1935. Beal was an attorney who had earned considerable wealth from land speculation and
industrial projects. He argued for federal law based on both the commerce clause of the Constitution and English common law. He ad-

vocated for federal law that specified exactly what pharmacists would be legally permitted to do with drug products as property. Kremers insisted that any law follow from and perpetuate the discoveries of experimental science. Cooperative manufacturing and bureaucratic state-level management should minimize profit from commercial trading. To Kremers, law and commerce are reformed by science sponsored by government. Beal held a more complex formulation. Property rights formed the social basis of law, commerce, and science. Any reformation of standards cannot violate any producer's right to ownership.

These philosophical differences suggest why Beal and Kremers were opposed to each other on the issues of price maintenance and the Tugwell Bill. Beal believed that price maintenance was important because it allowed groups of pharmacists to set common charges and reduce destructive competition. Kremers did not believe in the importance of price maintenance at all; money spent on lobbying was better spent on scientific research. Beal felt that the Tugwell Bill was an attempt by the federal government to usurp control of pharmaceutical standards from professional bodies. Kremers probably felt that government needed to intervene to remedy the shortcomings both before and after the Pure Food and Drugs Act. Their leadership and relationship helped to set the direction for pharmacy education and legislation in the twentieth century.

Notes

1.   Correspondence used for this paper is in the Kremers Reference Files at the University of Wisconsin Madison School of Pharmacy under the heading A2: Beal, J. H., hereafter KRF.
2.   Beal, 1916, written to W. Bodimer at Urbana, IL, KRF.
3.   Silverson, 1988.
4.   Griffenhagen, Blockstein, and Krigstein, 1994: 11-15 and 53-57.
5.   Young, 1974.
6.   Jackson, 1970: 215.
7.   Marks, 1997: 41.
8.   Bakalar, 1984: 94-95.
9.   For explanation of the British context and an alternative viewpoint regarding the adequacy of the medical/legal dichotomy, see Berridge, 1990: 101-114. The authors concluded that the penal/medical dichotomy is inadequate as an explanatory framework. Also Bakalar and Grinspoon, 1984: 69-76.
10.   Dupree, 1957: 256-301.
11.   Young, 1967.
12.   Anderson and Higby, 1995.
13.   This committee was formed by the American Public Health Association to address infant food and formula issues.

14. Kremers, 1940: 78.
15. This group included Lyman Kebler, who was also on AMA's Council on Pharmacy and Chemistry, Federal Specifications Board, and USP's Committee of Revision.
16. Stewart, 1901: 1177.
17. Stewart's company was a non-profit, private share company incorporated in New Jersey. Articles of incorporation as well as his correspondence to Robert Fischelis regarding pharmacy's place relative to medicine, law, and theology are found in the Francis E. Stewart papers, Historical Society of Wisconsin, Madison, WI, Box 7, Folder 6.
18. Higby, 1992: 20.
19. Ibid., 91.
20. Wiley, 1930.
21. Robinson-Patman Act, 15 U.S.C., § 13a, 13b, 21 (1937).
22. Not just narcotics. The Pure Food and Drugs Act of 1906 specifically mentioned any drug with known "habit-forming" potential including compounds like acetanilide. Martin I. Wilbert (1915: 55-57) discussed the government's perspective on the problem of intoxication from habit-forming substances.
23. Kremers, 1940: 61-79.
24. James Hartley Beal to Edward Kremers, 14 June 1895, KRF.
25. Beal to Kremers, 3 July 1895.
26. Beal, 1910.
27. For the official history of the American Association of Colleges of Pharmacy, see Buerki, 1999: 17-46 (Fall Supplement).
28. Beal to Kremers, 7 April 1898.
29. Beal to Kremers, 11 October 1902.
30. Beal to Kremers, 11 October 1902.
31. KRF: A2, Beal, J. H.
32. Beal to Kremers, 29 September 1903.
33. Beal to Kremers, 26 February 1907.
34. Beal, 1916, "Partial confession."
35. Sonnedecker, 1986: 555.
36. E. Kremers to J. P. Remington, n.d., c. 1910.
37. Wiley resigned according to his autobiographical account.
38. C. A. Mayo, Telegram to E. Kremers, 20 March 1912.
39. R. A. Badger to Vice President J. S. Sherman, 18 March 1912.
40. R. A. Badger to E. Kremers, 2 April 1912.
41. G. B. Kauffman to E. Kremers, 27 March 1912.
42. E. Kremers to President Taft, 20 March 1912.
43. President Taft's secretary to Kremers, 1 April 1912.
44. Beal to Kremers, 25 March 1912.
45. Beal to Kremers, 29 March 1912.
46. Beal to Kremers, 21 February 1916.
47. The 1914 Smith-Lever Act established an Agricultural Experiment Station at each land grant college. Land grant colleges were part of the Morrill Act of 1862, the enabling legislation that established the Department of Agriculture and the Department of Chemistry.
48. Kremers to Beal, 29 February 1916.
49. Beal to Kremers, 3 July 1917.
50. Kremers to Beal, 25 November 1918.
51. G. D. Beal to Kremers, 5 July 1917.
52. Kremers to G. D. Beal, 11 July 1917.
53. Beal to Kremers, 29 August 1918.

54. Kremers to Beal, 31 October 1918.
55. Beal to Kremers, 12 November 1918.
56. E. Kremers, James H. Beal: personal reflection, n.d., c. 1922.
57. Mason, 1901: 150-151.
58. "Alcohol Committee Organized" (1923), *Pharmaceutical Era 56* (6): 730.
59. Beal, 1916: 1251; Beal, 1920: 357-360; Beal, 1926.
60. Correspondence with the LaFollette family is found in the Edward Kremers Papers, Wisconsin Historical Society, Archives Division, Madison, WI, Box 9, Folder 3.
61. Beal to Kremers, 7 July 1919.
62. Beal to Kremers, 28 May 1919.
63. Kremers to Beal, 6 June 1919.
64. Kremers to Beal, 6 June 1919.
65. Beal to Kremers, 21 January 1920.
66. Beal to Kremers, 30 September 1920.
67. Beal to Kremers, 15 October 1921.
68. Kremers to Beal, 19 October 1921.
69. Beal to Kremers, 25 October 1921.
70. Kremers, James H. Beal: personal reflection, n.d., c. 1922.
71. Kremers to Secretary Henry, 8 January 1923.
72. Beal to Kremers, 25 January 1923
73. Beal to Kremers, 23 November 1925.
74. A. G. Bagley to Kremers, 26 November 1924.
75. Kremers to Beal, 5 December 1924; Beal to Kremers, 8 December 1924; Kremers to Beal, 20 May 1926; Beal to Kremers, 31 May 1926; Kremers to Beal 3 June 1926.
76. Beal to Bagley, 8 June 1926.
77. Beal to Kremers, 8 June 1926.
78. Kremers to Beal, 29 July 1930.
79. Beal to Kremers, 9 August 1930.
80. Ibid.
81. Kremers to Beal, 13 August 1930.
82. Beal to Kremers, 4 September 1930.
83. Ibid.
84. Beal to Kremers, 21 January 1934.
85. Beal to Kremers, 15 March 1934.
86. Most of the correspondence that Kremers kept in Beal's A2 file was from Beal. Kremers kept few letters he wrote to Beal in this file.
87. Beal, 1895: 331-332.
88. Parascandola, 1995: 156-167.

4

Dispensing Doctors and
Counter-Prescribing Pharmacists

Chapter 3, "Letters between Leaders," discussed the nature of codification efforts through education and legislation. The purpose of this codification was to elevate the professional practices of "rank and file" practitioners in medicine and pharmacy. From their fifty-year personal correspondence, James Hartley Beal and Edward Kremers were presented as two prominent educators who contributed to and led professionalization through law and science.

In this chapter, conflicting views of pharmaceutical fact and professional propriety surrounding the practices of dispensing physicians and counter-prescribing pharmacists are examined. In addition, the professional groups that claimed jurisdiction over the standards of an evolving array of pharmaceutical substances and products are highlighted. Corporate philanthropy financed many social reform programs during the period aimed at curbing the impact of fraud and vice on the American public.

This chapter will focus on the activities and interpretations of an outside observer, the American Social Hygiene Association (ASHA), with reference to efforts by state and federal governments to control the incidence and prevalence of venereal diseases.[1] Started in 1914, the American Social Hygiene Association (now the American Social Health Association) was founded by prominent philanthropists, including John D. Rockefeller, Jr., Grace H. and Cleveland H. Dodge, and Felix M. Warburg. William F. Snow, M.D., of California, was its first executive director. In 1943, APhA executive secretary Robert P.

Based on a presentation to the Second Session of the American Institute of the History of Pharmacy, American Pharmaceutical Association sesquicentennial annual meeting in Philadelphia, 19 March 2002.

Fischelis was elected to the Board of Directors of ASHA. Correspondence between Snow and Fischelis began in 1918 over nostrums for venereal disease treatment.[2]

A Haphazard Drug Therapy System

Despite governmental and professional efforts to negotiate pharmaceutical fact through rational therapeutics and pharmacopoeial scope, the American Social Hygiene Association observed the widespread disregard for standards and statutes by producers and consumers of drug therapy alike. In their view, a haphazard system for the drug therapy of venereal disease was a major threat to the entire population. ASHA officials believed that enforcement of medical practice, pharmacy, and public health laws at the state level would shape a responsive drug therapy system, and provide economic incentives for producers and consumers to address the medical aspects of the menace of venereal diseases.

Stopping short of federal control, ASHA argued for reform within the existing structure that influenced and governed professional practices. According to ASHA, a relatively developed division of labor already existed on which to base any enforcement decisions to arbitrate the will of both "producers" and "consumers." ASHA advocated for the separation of pharmaceutical therapies into prescription and non-prescription entities because the public should seek the advice and prescriptions of qualified physicians for treatment of gonorrhea and syphilis. Treatment of venereal disease should commence only after a face-to-face diagnosis by a scientifically trained, allopathic physician with prescriptions directed to competent pharmacists.

One of the goals of the Pure Food and Drugs Act was to regulate the ubiquitous nostrum trade. Before the discovery and widespread distribution of sulfonamides, venereal disease was treated largely with nostrums of many kinds. The Act vested legal authority in the rubrics of the USP and the NF, and conferred official status to the names of listed articles. As suggested by James Hartley Beal, the "variation clause" allowed manufacturers to continue to sell products that were not "official," provided the label specified the deviation from the USP article.[3] Moreover, the law pertained only to articles transported across state lines. The Act, therefore, did not cover all articles used in professional practice or sold in commercial exchange, and allowed the nostrum trade to proliferate for venereal disease treatments.

The USP included only non-proprietary products of the materia medica. As committee of one appointed for the purpose of transmitting the views of the American Pharmaceutical Association, F. E. Stewart, Ph.G., M.D., testified on the subject of patents and trademarks to the U.S. Congress. He said: [4]

> The wishes of this Association [APhA] are that Congress shall so revise the patent law as to exclude materia medica products from patent protection, and so revise the trademark law that the currently used names of materia medica products shall be refused registration.... The great reason why we object as pharmacists to any method whereby control is secured over the manufacture and sale of materia medica products is because it enables quacks to reap a harvest by misleading the people. Throw the products open to legitimate competition, and the nostrum business would soon become unprofitable.... The evils of this business were not so apparent to the pharmaceutical profession so long as pharmacists made money by handling advertised package goods over their counter. But the advent of the cutter fortunately opened the eyes of many pharmacists to the great danger threatening the pharmaceutical profession from the encroachments of the unlicensed practitioner.... The true object of the trademark law is to protect the public from counterfeit brand marks, so that people may be able to discriminate between the various makes of articles of commerce.

Moreover, the NF contained formulae in common use among pharmacists and physicians.[5] Both USP and NF excluded synthetic and proprietary articles. For biological injections, such as diphtheria antitoxin and arsphenamine, USP standards were derived from the Surgeon General's office of the United States Public Health Service through the Hygienic Laboratory.[6] To quote USP XII:[7]

> Arsphenamine must be prepared in an establishment licensed for that purpose by the United States Government upon recommendation of the Surgeon General of the United States Public Health Service. Each lot of the product, before being offered for sale must comply with the toxicity, labeling, and other requirements of the National Institute of Health and be released by the Institute. Antitoxicum Diphthericum—United States Pharmacopoeia XII.

Again:[8]

> Diphtheria antitoxin complies with the requirements of the National Institute of Health of the United States Public Health Service. Vaccinum Rabies—United States Pharmacopoeia XII. Rabies vaccine complies with the requirements of the National Institute of Health of the United States Public Health Service.

To address the standards for proprietary formulations omitted in official compendia, the American Medical Association created the Council on Pharmacy and Chemistry (CPC). While CPC dealt with synthetic drugs, like heroin, two of its members (Puckner and Steiglitz from Chicago) served on another group that formed after World War

I, the National Research Council's Division of Chemistry and Chemical Technology. Created in 1919, the Division's main purpose was to advise the Federal Trade Commission (FTC) on questions relating to licenses for the manufacture of synthetic drugs, especially those with patents held by German companies, and to determine the means to encourage domestic production. The committee on synthetic drugs of the division of chemistry and chemical technology was founded on 25 March 1919. Its purpose was to serve as official advisor to FTC on questions relating to licenses for the manufacture of synthetic drugs. Members included: Julius Stieglitz, University of Chicago; Francis M. Phelps; Moses Gomberg; G. W. McCoy; Edward S. Rogers; and William A. Puckner, Council on Pharmacy and Chemistry, American Medical Association. According to a memo from committee leader Bancroft:[9]

> Functions of the committee: (1) to act in an advisory capacity in matters relating to the chemistry of synthetic drugs and their manufacture; (2) to initiate research on problems connected with synthetic drugs; (3) to take the initiative in securing the manufacture in America of important synthetic drugs; and (4) to study the tests employed for identity and purity of drugs and to cooperate with other agencies, such as the Council on Pharmacy and Chemistry and the American Medical Association, in this connection.

In short, definitions and standards were both publicly and privately derived and arbitrated. The universe of pharmaceutical therapies divided into two mutually exclusive, producer-oriented categories—official preparations and all others. U.S. Public Health Service pharmacist Martin. I. Wilbert summarized Division of Drugs Chief Lyman F. Kebler's remarks about the pharmacopoeial process.[10]

> In discussing the desirability of restricting the number of drugs used, [he] points out that the Pharmacopoeia is the law and standard, but that with the present construction of the law, he is inclined to wish that there was no Pharmacopoeia.

Official preparations could be so labeled and sold only if all the production requirements of the USP were met. Resulting from the 1902 Biologics Control Act, the Hygienic Laboratory determined the standards for biological products in the USP.[11] New and nonofficial remedies were evaluated by the Council on Pharmacy and Chemistry, and published in the *Propaganda for Reform*. The American Pharmaceutical Association's National Formulary Committee made available uniform recipes for preparing consistent formulations of non-commercialized products. Often, while the professional groups encountered overlapping purviews when it came to establishment of standards, these three groups constituted the professional structure for pharmaceutical fact.

While state laws often specified the details of prescribing and dispensing within state borders, federal law was silent on what would be done in actual practice. Wilbert commented on the relations between the professions when he wrote that "the relations existing between pharmacists and physicians are in an unsatisfactory and altogether unsettled condition."[12] USP standards were written to assure the place of individual compounding. The products of any manufacturer were considered genuine articles of medical and commercial trade provided they did not claim or imply any curative properties in their product name or label.

One of the goals of the Council on Pharmacy and Chemistry was to eliminate secret formulas held by manufacturers: If companies desired recommendation of their products by physicians and pharmacists, the contents had to be divulged. Operated by pharmacist William A. Puckner, the Committee on Chemistry provided analytical reports of patent medicines to support Council pronouncements. In this way, therapies marketed only to physicians became separated from those advertised directly to the public. The manufacturer decided which of these audiences would be solicited and whether their product would require a prescription. Organized medicine was against professional recommendation without full knowledge of the product's constituents: Organized pharmacy was against dispensing potent therapies without a physician's prescription.

After the First World War, practical and organizational conflicts between physicians and pharmacists centered on the scientific basis for the initiation and handling of drug therapy. Organizational leaders in pharmacy were content to leave therapeutic questions to physicians: Pharmacists interested in making a living often compounded and/or recommended therapies without the benefit of a physician's diagnosis. Physicians often dispensed pharmaco-therapeutic intervention knowing little about product make-up. "Counter-prescribing" pharmacists and "dispensing" doctors were opposite sides of the same empirical coin: Both sold products with little regard for medical reasoning and without charging for their service. Deeply rooted in professional history, these practices by each group were indicative of a lower class of practitioner. As early as 1852, pharmacists and physicians banded together to jointly denounce the quackery of nostrum sales within their ranks. At that formative time, it was reported: [13]

> All that the best disposed apothecary can be expected to do, is to refrain from the
> manufacture himself of quack and secret medicines; to abstain from recommending
> them, either verbally or by exhibiting show bills, announcing them for sale; and to
> discourage their use, when appealed to.

Later, many physicians and pharmacists held that pharmacy was
a legitimate branch of medicine. Ezra Hunt of Nebraska held that
"the first step in remedying this evil [nostrum sales] must be to hold
pharmacy to accountability and reliability, by making it a part of the
profession of medicine."[14] Hunt wrote:[15]

> Prescribing pharmacists abound. The prescriptions of physicians are used with free-
> dom, and are repeated indefinitely without the knowledge of the prescriber...which is
> antagonistic to the principle of individual prescription for each case.... Place the dispen-
> sary in its natural relation, in charge of a member of the medical profession by choice
> assigned to that department, and society would be shielded from exposure to irrespon-
> sible remedies, and from the temptation to self-medication to which, by the present
> system, it is constantly and cordially invited.... The pharmacist, within the fold where
> he legitimately belonged, would have the status demanded by therapeutics, and would
> thereby become directly interested with other physicians in the advance of our art....
> Therapeutics, adjusting the relation between diagnosis and cure, has the right to claim
> such a union.... Instead of leaving the pharmacist outside, let us invite him within the
> boundaries of the legitimate practice, and let him become imbued with the *esprit de
> corps* which belongs to a noble profession.

The sentiment continued as James England, chairman of the APhA
section on education and legislation commented, "Pharmacy is a
branch of therapeutics." He said:[16]

> Strictly speaking, pharmacy is a branch of therapeutics. It is as much a medical branch
> as dental surgery is a branch of general surgery.... Is the possibility of scientific
> pharmacy an iridescent dream, or not? Or, has the plan of Prof. George H. Meeker, who
> urges the creation of "certified clinical chemists" for clinical chemistry work, under the
> auspices of the American Pharmaceutical Association and the American Medical Asso-
> ciation, serious possibilities?

To these professional leaders, the quackery situation existed, in
large part, because of the artificial separation and distinction between the two disciplines. If integrated as one profession, with oversight by medicine, pharmacy would achieve professional status
through the science of therapeutics. Conflicts would be handled in-
ternally instead of in public.

In addition to counter-prescribing pharmacists and dispensing
doctors, organized medicine and pharmacy faced equally threatening challenges from what they considered non-standards-based practices: Unlicensed "health" practitioners and unsanctioned pharmaceutical products. Social activists in and outside of medicine and

pharmacy perceived these practices as a threat to public health, and joined with physicians and pharmacists in the AMA to combat the "quackery" situation.

The idea of quackery derives from fraud. Fraud was a major basis of the Pure Food and Drugs Act of 1906, and was codified as adulteration and misbranding. The 1906 Act, as amended, was not adequate for medicalizing all pharmaceutical use by citizens. It was designed to define what circumstances would be actionable by the federal government for items sold in interstate commerce. What was considered genuine and quack regarding persons was within a state's jurisdiction. Although fraud related to tangible commodities was actionable at the federal level, fraud related to services was not. Federal authorities were involved in quackery only to the extent that the mail was used to solicit business and transport goods across state borders.

In the prevailing attitude of the Progressive years, the good citizen needed outside, informed advice for the proper use of pharmaceutical therapies. Good practitioners of medicine based their advice on rational therapeutics, and sent pharmaceutical prescriptions to good pharmacists who, within their scope, compounded and dispensed in accordance with pharmacopoeial standards codified in the law.[17] Physician Horatio C. Wood wrote:[18]

> Twenty-five years ago there were doctors prescribing advertised nostrums and rarely writing extemporaneous prescriptions…the physician can aid pharmacy…by selecting an apothecary in whose competence and integrity confidence may be reposed, and diverting as large a proportion of his prescription work to this one pharmacist…by taking a public stand against the encroachments of the chain-store system…by discouraging the use of nostrums and self-medication…to regenerate a professional spirit…pharmacy is not only the handmaiden, but also the offspring of medicine.

In an accompanying response in the journal, *International Clinics*, pharmacy leader Charles LaWall commented:[19]

> [Physicians] form their judgment of pharmacy, as a rule, by the erroneous conclusions that may easily be drawn from a hasty glance at some modern drug stores…prescription writing is so inadequately taught in the medical colleges at the present time…. The dispensing doctor is far more common today than the prescribing pharmacist…practice medicine in the proper manner by writing prescriptions for the individual needs of each patient… the trained pharmacist gets the difficult jobs…. He stands ready to dispense official drugs, chemicals, and preparations prescribed for the individual needs of the particular case instead of supplying ready-made prescriptions introduced by clever detail men (usually physicians or pharmacists who have entered this field of work), often furnished in package form ready to hand out to the patient…. There are some common enemies against which warfare should be waged, shoulder to shoulder, by physicians and

pharmacists…the spread of those cults…therapeutic nihilism…exploitation of unnecessary proprietary medicines… We need a new and joint code of ethics in which shall be embodied the principles of common responsibility and opportunity for service.

These leaders envisioned a system that would control the potential for vice generated by unscrupulous manufacturers as well as by a citizen's improper choices and their desires to have a more satisfying future state of being. The system for professionally directed drug therapy had a major ramification on the rights of citizens in a free society: It would stop citizens from acting in their best interest, and would shift consequent responsibility to professionals and to government. A complicating factor, according to Janssen, was that, at the time, "the same drugs were being labeled with directions by some manufacturers and with the Prescription Legend by others, sometimes both ways by the same firm."[20]

Problems Presented by Venereal Disease

Along with narcotic habituation, alcoholism, and tuberculosis, many in government and the military perceived venereal disease as important, pervasive, and menacing public health problems of post-World War I America. In a 1929 *Bulletin of Pharmacy* (a widely circulated pharmacist newsletter of the time), Surgeon-General H. S. Cummings reiterated the government's stance on venereal disease after enactment of the Chamberlain-Kahn Act of 1917:[21]

One of the great public health problems which confronts all the authorities of the country is the prevention and control of the venereal diseases…. In 1918-1919 as a part of the venereal disease control program of the Public Health Service, an appeal was sent to 48,500 retail druggists in the United States asking them: (1) Not to prescribe or recommend any remedy for a venereal disease; (2) not to purchase any proprietary remedy to be sold to the public for self-treatment of a venereal disease and not to sell any such remedy after January 15, 1919; (3) to refill only such prescriptions for the treatment of venereal diseases as were given originally to the customer by a reputable physician who is still in charge of the case; (4) to distribute literature furnished by the Public Health Service to persons asking, without a physician's prescription, for remedies customarily confined to the treatment of venereal disease, and to direct such persons to a reputable physician, to an approved clinic, or to the State board of health…28,226, or nearly 60 per cent, of the druggists agreed voluntarily to cooperate with the Public Health Service in the manner requested…. No reputable pharmacist will knowingly aid in providing a patient with material for such self-treatment…. Through a wise provision of Congress, which became effective in 1902, the supervision of the sale of all biological products for use in the treatment of human beings was placed under the direction of the Public Health Service.

Despite the discovery of arsphenamine and its cogeners by German scientist Robert Ehrlich in 1909, drug therapy for syphilis and gonorrhea remained largely haphazard and ineffective. The Dermatological Research Laboratories in Philadelphia and the state health departments of New York and Massachusetts received post-war licenses to market German synthetic drugs, including arsphenamine, from the Federal Trade Commission. Not surprising, many different kinds of treatments—drug and non-drug—were offered for sale by trained professionals and laity alike. That venereal disease had identifiable microbiological causes, physiopathological sequelae, and pharmacological treatments were transmitted through the United States Public Health Service's journal, *Venereal Disease Information*, beginning in 1919. As science provided a firmer basis for biomedical decision making and intervention, public health workers and government officials became more certain that their actions to control the spread of venereal disease could be justified in light of evolving empirical evidence.

Narcotics and alcohol became the objects of federal efforts to control vice, first through taxation, then outright prohibition, of interstate commerce. Although woven into the fabric of vice, control of tuberculosis and venereal disease was not so bureaucratically crafted. In fact, venereal disease was so tied to private family and treatment issues that its social management, to be effective, had to remain local in scope. Thus, many large cities, like New York, Chicago, Newark, New Orleans, and Kansas City, enacted local ordinances that governed venereal disease identification, treatment, and eradication efforts within their jurisdictions. While many state boards of health required the reporting of infected and treated individuals, as early as 1911 by Snow in California,[22] these mandates were not enforceable. There were simply too many infected and too many "practitioners" to follow.

Moreover, because latent stages of syphilis and gonorrhea could be misjudged as remission or cure, it was difficult to determine and justify who should be monitored by the state through public health departments. Existing law regarding medical or pharmaceutical practices, commerce and trade, or contagious disease reporting, whether local or state in scope, was not followed voluntarily by the professions or enforced uniformly by government.

While the success of these local control efforts was tenuous in light of economic conditions around the Great Depression, their discussion contributed to an evolving social thought on a formalized drug therapy sanctioning system. Efforts to provide systematic identification of venereal disease by qualified (and controllable) practitioners using scientifically validated treatments from reputable (and controllable) sources led to the development of a social system of medical sanctions. These sanctions provided the context for appropriate actions by citizens and practitioners—treatment of venereal disease—that may have become a precursor to organized government control of an official system of prescribing and dispensing.

The Results of Field Surveys of Drugstores

The American Social Hygiene Association became a leading exponent and arbiter of societal propriety. Alarmed about the threat of mistreated venereal, ASHA conducted a series of field surveys in major United States cities to determine the extent, causes, and treatments of syphilis and gonorrhea, particularly from minority segments such as immigrant Europeans and Negroes. These surveys identified a multitude of disease identification, treatment, and follow-up problems leading to and perpetuating the exploitation of the ignorant by unscrupulous "practitioners." In their view, the root of the problem was the fact that potentially infected persons could choose whose advice and treatment would be sought to remedy their disease within their own means. ASHA described the spontaneous "system" that developed due to the influence of advertising, and the methods and nomenclature inherent in that system of treatment.

Arguing that care from duly licensed physicians provided the only meaningful form of therapy, assertions of miraculous cures for vague conditions like "blood or nervous disorders" or "lost manhood" were tantamount to fraud and deception. Charlatans actually stimulated seminal exudation by the prostatic massage of many men, a normal physiological response to tactile pressure, which was given as positive substantial evidence of serious, chronic, and deep-seated gonorrhea requiring immediate attention from them.

Moreover, field studies showed that physical examination of the complainant was not necessary to receive a treatment or remedy. Face-to-face interviews of retail druggists (presumably licensed by the state) and so called "quacks" by ASHA operatives posing as "patients" revealed a variety of techniques used to instill fear, enlist confidence, and extract long-term financial contracts with "patients." Newspaper ads promised hope, and usually a cure, for those who had tried "Doctors, Professors, and Reverends." Mail order and tele-

phone mechanisms conveyed treatments for the patient's self-described symptomatology at a distance. An in-person visit was not
required; ability to pay was.

The Impropriety of Self-Treatment

Amid the social and medical chaos surrounding venereal disease,
what, then, was the mission of ASHA relative to drug therapy control? Clearly, any form of self-treatment for venereal disease was a
delusion and danger, and anyone servicing, perpetuating, and prof-
iting from that delusion was a quack. "The proper treatment of [gon-
orrhea and syphilis] requires expert handling by a specially trained
physician," a regimen where "certain drugs which require difficult
techniques to administer must be carefully adjusted to the patient's
physical condition and progress of his disease."[23] At the time of the
investigation, however, many regular physicians lacked the skill to
make an intravenous injection of mercurials or arsenicals.[24] The "specially trained physician" was not only one versed in venereal disease identification, but also in the techniques of invasive treatment
administration required by arsphenamine and mercurials. ASHA was
concerned about the need for medical follow-up and quarantine:
Typically, a series of intravenous or intramuscular injections, combined with topical irrigation or unction, was required to affect a
change in the disease's presentation.

Moreover, the types and results of therapies offered from around
the world probably did little to bolster ASHA operatives' confidence
of effective treatment by private physicians and counter-prescribing
pharmacists. Reports from the United States and abroad showed a
variety of substances and administration techniques used in clinical
treatments. Therapeutic strategies for gonorrhea ranged from drugless,
"constitutional" regimens (involving quiet, a simple diet, and copi-
ous fluids), prostatic massage, and diathermy to drug therapies involving internal and external potassium salts (primarily citrate, io-
dine, and permanganate), intravenously injected pooled serum for-
tified with arsphenamine, urethral gauze inserts containing 3 percent silver nitrate (Protargol©), topical application of soothing san-
dalwood oil and sulfur, and intramuscular injections of acriflavine
and sulfarsphenamin.[25] Laymen and non-professionals did not only
concern ASHA about venereal disease treatment. There was a corollary threat from the unstandardized treatments offered by regular,
private (untrained) physicians and pharmacists.

Thus, several groups were targeted for the investigation of sub-standard drug therapy: Those who advertised "pseudo-therapeutic" (meaning unlicensed) services, referred to as quacks (herbalists, charlatans, evil-eye specialists, professors, reverends, yogis, and fortune tellers); and those who traded in venereal disease treatments with the appearance of license from the state like druggists, pharmacists, doctors, institutes, and physicians. Several characteristic practices were indicative of quackery to social hygiene advocates. Anyone who advocated self-treatment of syphilis and gonorrhea "willfully deceives and lies in order to exploit the patient."[26]

Many patients susceptible to this delusion were disillusioned by orthodox treatment, and these "cases given up by other physicians as incurable are especially solicited."[27] Many quacks were quick to capitalize on the ethnic mix of Chicago, offering therapeutic approaches that ministered to culturally ingrained beliefs and values. Often, "practitioners" exploited patients of their own heritage or race. "They assume such titles as 'Reverend,' 'Professor,' 'Doctor,' and 'Yogi' in order to impress their victims. These charlatans include ignorant Negroes, East Indians, and some white persons."[28] It was not clear whether the term, "venereal disease" was even in the vocabulary, let alone the vernacular, of ethnic peoples of the time. "Many newspapers for Negroes and foreign-language groups still carry advertisements of 'blood specialists,' 'lost manpower remedies,' and other 'cures.' Usually the advertisements are couched in guarded terms and often no mention is made of venereal disease."[29] A Hungarian newspaper published an advertisement for a health institute claiming to exist for "repression of quackery…to save the Hungarian people from being robbed by quacks, this institution has been established for the purpose of providing them with the right kind of treatment."[30]

Quacks and charlatans were classified by ASHA into one of three types:

> (1) Pseudo "specialists for men," "specialists of blood disease," "health institutes," and "medical offices" who reach their clients through newspaper advertisements, pamphlets, and circulars distributed on the streets and other public places; (2) Herbalists, witchcraft "professors," "evil-eye specialists," Hindu yogis, fortune tellers and other fakers, who advertise and offer to treat in person or through the mail; and (3) Remedy companies and individuals who advertise and offer to sell remedies for the self-treatment and cure of "blood-disease," "lost man power,' and other sexual conditions.[31]

What was clear to ASHA was that the subcultures of major United States cities actually supported a diversity of scientific, mystical, and practical approaches to disease treatment. These approaches included tapping into "primitive" forms of knowing nature within the milieu of a direct (barter) and indirect (cash) economy. And, according to ASHA, there was only one true way to know the nature of disease: the application of scientific principles of identification and systematic treatment by certified medical experts. But, the existing law in Chicago was inadequate for stopping self-proclaimed specialty for treating and curing venereal disease. "There seems to be no adequate law on the Illinois statute books which specifically forbids this type of quack from advertising as a specialist, or from announcing that he treats and cures syphilis and gonorrhea."[32]

While ASHA associated drugstore "counter-prescribing" by pharmacists with quackery by laymen and quasi-doctors, they did not label pharmacists as quacks. Moreover, ASHA did not call what quacks did counter-prescribing. Counter-prescribing is a deeply seated, culturally acceptable form of advice-giving with roots in the empirical method, and ASHA wanted pharmacists to be part of their solution to quackery and unorthodox and illegal treatment practices. "The study shows that the members of the pharmaceutical profession are in a strategic position to aid or hinder any movement for the prevention and proper treatment of the venereal diseases."[33] There was great interest in appealing to the voluntary cooperation between pharmacists and physicians to extinguish self-treatment of venereal disease fostered by counter-prescribing and dispensing nostrums. Meetings between the two groups were often recommended "to discuss ways and means to revive the agreement made during the [First] World War by individual druggists not to counter-prescribe for or sell remedies for the self-treatment of the venereal diseases."[34]

Through the Chamberlain-Kahn Act of 1917, the Public Health Service enlisted the support of pharmacists to refrain from counter-prescribing, but it was obvious that a gentleman's agreement was insufficient for maintaining these practices during peacetime. However, ASHA seemed to appreciate the pharmacists' economic circumstances as well as their local availability in Chicago and other major cities.

> Frequently, persons infected with syphilis or gonorrhea, not realizing the seriousness of these diseases, apply to pharmacists for advice or a remedy to cure their condition. This is especially true among certain foreign-language and Negro groups.[35]

For many pharmacists, treatment of venereal disease constituted a major portion of their business. However, not even half of these retail pharmacists were members of the Chicago Retail Druggists' Association. As a group, they were difficult to mobilize because their business motives seemed contradictory. There were a number of cut-rate stores where usually no prescriptions were filled. Physicians did not regularly send patients to pharmacists for medicines. Many pharmacists sold a variety of articles, and became complex merchandising agencies, restaurants, and ice cream parlors. Many practicing physicians stocked various drugs and even compound their own prescriptions. Mail order houses sold remedies as well. This was "pointed out for the purpose of indicating the difficulties some of the druggists encounter in their endeavor to pay expenses and make a fair profit."[36] It could be argued, then, that channeling prescription patients from physicians to pharmacists would differentiate them from other sources of supply. If pharmacists would give up counter-prescribing by referring patients to physicians, physicians would give up compounding and dispensing treatments.

Quackery in Major United States Cities

In Chicago, home of the American Medical Association, efforts to expose unscientific treatment by unqualified persons was aimed at establishing allopathic medicine as the standard bearer of rational therapeutics. Venereal disease may have been the first therapeutic area where statues governed access to drug therapy. The *Chicago Tribune* worked with AMA and local social hygiene advocates in a ten-year quackery campaign from 1915 to 1926.[37] Kansas City, Missouri, and New Orleans had stricter municipal ordinances and state laws than Chicago. For example, the Charter and revised ordinances of Kansas City, Missouri, in 1928 provided very specific instructions on what was expected from physicians, pharmacists, and others when suspecting a venereal disease case.

> The patient would be furnished with a circular of information and advice concerning venereal diseases furnished by the Director of Health, and in addition to give to such diseased person a copy of this article relating to venereal diseases, and to report to the Director of Health that such diseased person has received the two documents specified herein.[38]

The law required an auditable treatment trail showing which physician and/or other persons treated any individual patient.[39] The director of health could quarantine any person with known or suspected venereal disease, which in Kansas City during this time could mean a hospital stay of over fifty days. Only physicians approved by the director could see patients while in isolation.[40] The public health law required druggists to keep sales records of persons applying with prescriptions from licensed physicians for treatment, but were prohibited from any independent actions to remedy anyone's complaints without expressed written authorization in the form of a signed order.[41]

> No druggist or other person not a physician licensed under the laws of the state shall prescribe or recommend to any person any drugs, medicines, or other substance to be used for the cure or alleviation of gonorrhea, syphilis, or chancroid, or shall compound any drugs or medicines for such purpose from any written formula or order not written for the person for whom the drugs or medicines are compounded and not signed by a physician licensed under the laws of the state.[42]

The effect of this section was clear. Proper treatment started with the physician; no deviation in any form or for any purpose was permitted. The mechanisms established in these ordinances may have facilitated a sanctioning system applicable to all drug therapy on a broader scale.

However, tighter ordinances did not necessarily lead to better control of counter-prescribing, quackery, and nostrum selling on the request of would-be patients. "The conditions in Kansas City regarding quackery and 'counter-prescribing' are not satisfactory. Better laws and better law enforcement are suggested."[43] Estimates of the prevalence of syphilis and gonorrheas in Kansas City in 1934 were syphilis 5 percent, and gonorrhea 10-15 percent of its population. The annual expenditure for medical care was estimated at about $1 million.[44] Because of the magnitude of the problem, ASHA seemed to use a more systematic survey method in Kansas City to illustrate clearly the deficiencies of current local statutes.

In comparison to Chicago, the municipal ordinances of Kansas City pertaining to venereal disease control were more directive and specific in terms of the sanctioned social structure of treatment. Sale of medicines required an individualized, signed prescription order from a licensed physician. Still, ASHA found it "a peculiarity of Kansas City that osteopaths are legally permitted to treat syphilis by the administration of drugs, a prerogative reserved in most states to physicians."[45] (ASHA did not study DOs). The director of health had broad powers to quarantine, and it was a civic responsibility to report any suspicious citizens.

Autonomous judgment by pharmacists was specifically prohibited by local statute. However, what ASHA found was that a majority of pharmacists continued to make diagnoses, offer remedies, and did not refer patients to physicians. The Kansas City records provided the only systematic file from the entire survey of drugstores in these major United States cities. As a group, pharmacists in Kansas City most often sold a remedy based on patient's description of symptoms, not on prescription. Further, pharmacists who sold a remedy usually did not advise the patient to seek a physician. Only 20 percent of pharmacists promised a cure for the patient's self-described disease. That pharmacists were not making promises of cure may have separated them as a group from so-called charlatans even though pharmacists sold patent medicines as a major part of their livelihoods.

The analysis may reveal a basic assumption held by pharmacists. Venereal disease could not be cured by anyone with the current state of medical knowledge. Perhaps because of this, ASHA advanced the position that the best way to mitigate social morbidity and mortality was to advocate, within existing law, for clearer, formal divisions of medical labor that provided appropriate channels for disease treatment. Patients would go to allopathic specially trained physicians for diagnosis and prescriptions of remedy, and then to pharmacists for compounding and dispensing the written prescriptions.

In New Orleans, the Sanitary Code of Louisiana prohibited advertising and sale of a preparation for the prevention of venereal diseases, except on the written prescription of a physician. According to statute,

> No individual, firm, druggist, or manufacturing establishment shall mix, compound, sell, or advertise any preparation, ointment, injection or single drug for the purpose of preventing or affecting the prophylaxis of venereal diseases, except upon the written prescription of a licensed physician.[46]

Many creative practices were employed by pharmacists to meet the law's requirements, and statements by interviewed pharmacists were compiled by ASHA interviewers posing as patients that provide insight into the nature of the practices.

> Given temporary relief and advised to consult physician, or go to hospital or clinic.
> There appear to be a greater number of colored people making these requests and these are steadily increasing.
> We employ a physician and allow free consultation on Wednesdays and Saturdays for poor people. A great many are treated, if they have money to pay for the medicine; if not, they are referred to the charity hospitals. A great many apply who don't have the necessary money and of which we keep no record. A great many ask for H.G.C. and P_____ capsules. Every day, we sell on request by name, Balsam Copass, sweet spirits of nitre, etc., which we assume is for gonorrhea, altho not mentioned.

I counter prescribe and sometimes suggest a physician.

I find that during these conditions, the Pharmacist is asked to help the sick and depressed for advice before they call to see a Doctor. Of course, for Humanity's sake, if I can help an unfortunate, I give him or her what advice I can. If I think they need a doctor's advice, I send them to the Hospital. I find that most gonorrhea cases are women—young women that are just starting in womanhood. Most doctors call these conditions "leucorrhea" or "whites," which, in my opinion, is a mild form of gonorrhea.[47]

Some drug stores were conducting an extensive business in counter-prescribing for venereal disease. Others employed or provided office space for physicians with profits made from dispensing prescriptions divided between the pharmacist and physician. Others used the name of a physician as a cover for counter-prescribing in violation of Louisiana's Medical Practice Act.[48]

The practical problems between physicians and pharmacists were a special concern to ASHA. In East Harlem during the late 1920s, for example, ASHA estimated that about 25 percent of local pharmacists in an Italian district were practicing medicine illegally, despite city ordinances prohibiting sales without prescription. There were no laws that prohibited physicians in any jurisdiction from preparing and administering drug therapy. A survey of practitioners there reported that

The physicians in the district complain of the local pharmacists and some say that they are treating venereal disease patients illegally. Some of the druggists in turn claim that the physicians do not care to cooperate with them in sending prescriptions to them to be filled, and that the physicians have themselves to blame if some druggists have to resort to selling remedies behind the counter and treating patients. A few pharmacists even believe that they are doing a necessary charity by helping the poor, and some even think that they know how to treat venereal disease cases just as well as some of the practicing physicians. This trouble between the physicians and pharmacists seems to be based largely upon the economic conditions of making a living. A fair estimate is that 25 per cent of the local pharmacists in this district are violating the law in these respects.[49]

A Federally Mandated Drug Therapy System Was Needed

During the 1920s, private philanthropy and public health-minded physicians saw great advantages to a legally mandated system of drug therapy. Academic pharmacy was in favor of law that would place physicians' prescriptions in the hands of pharmacists and thereby reduce or eliminate pharmacists' financial dependence on the sale of non-drug merchandise. Because many physicians either did not write out their prescriptions or sold patent medicines, pharmacists often treated patients with venereal disease without referral to physicians in the established practice called "counter-prescribing." Advocating for a physician-directed drug therapy system, ASHA sought to improve relations between public health and private practice by making drug therapy the sole legal prerogative of physicians even though many could not administer treatments properly.

However, the "quackery" situation was similar in all parts of the country whether there were many exacting laws that governed the practice (New Orleans and Kansas City) or a few vague ones (Chicago, New York City, and Newark). Upholding AMA's idea of "quackery," ASHA sought to provide both evidence and polemic that would behoove local, state, and national authorities to enact stronger laws and enforce existing laws that sanctioned the initiation of pharmacotherapy only under certain circumstances. That context for therapy had several characteristics by default: (1) face-to-face dialogue between patient and allopathic physician; (2) no advertising or solicitation; (3) no mention or guarantees of cure; and (4) separate prescribing and dispensing activities specified by law.

Under existing law, no level of government could not ensure "pure" drugs recommended and administered as a therapeutic device by professionals who knew what they were doing. The federal government was able to enforce the medical context in which citizens received narcotics, and thereby control that aspect of the nostrum trade. James Hartley Beal had written: "the principal object of the law must be to prevent the creation of drug habits rather than reform those who are already enslaved." [50] Because of this sentiment toward preventing addiction rather than interfering with the supply of those that were already habituated, there were many preparations exempted from control through the Harrison Anti-Narcotic Act.

Use of narcotics under any other circumstances was illegal. Despite the efforts of Surgeon General Thomas Parran,[51] venereal disease control was only possible, and cure approachable, in the aftermath of the sulfanilamide tragedy by requiring the safety of pharmaceuticals. However, it is interesting to note that sulfonamides became the object of government efforts to enforce pre-market safety of drug products at the same time the sulfonamides offered a medical cure for venereal disease.[52]

Outside mechanisms of control of the therapeutic process became firmly institutionalized with narcotics, alcohol, and venereal diseases because of their connection with vice. The medical police concept had motivated many public health campaigns. However, by injecting police power into an evolving structure of medical authority over therapeutics, a false sense of propriety and security about drug therapy approved by government only magnified the weaknesses of individual responsibility, a fear that dominated Progressive-like reforms. Thus, venereal disease laws were not effective in addressing socially acceptable forms of treatment despite considerable advances in scientific therapies like neoarsphenamine. Arsenicals, however, were not sulfonamides, not in terms of safety, efficacy, and ease of administration.

Then-Secretary of Commerce Herbert Hoover who directed the federal government's commercial policies in the 1920s allowed businessmen and professionals to set their own standards of operation.[53] The Market Crash brought this policy into serious question. According to Wiebe:[54]

> A more elaborate and permissive federal government, serving as a clearinghouse for business compromise, widened the new communities of interest.... Considering the pressures of hard times, former progressives remained remarkably passive while successful businessmen worked with President Hoover to strengthen the self-regulatory system of the 1920s. As Hoover turned increasingly negative, more flexible business leaders, well before Franklin Roosevelt's inauguration, proposed the central idea of what would be the National Recovery Administration...they supplied the NRA with its basic substance, the codes.... When the New Deal after 1935 alienated most successful businessmen, the bulk of the old progressive groups either joined business leaders in protecting the establishment or sought neutral ground.

Government held standards-setting groups accountable for the standards they had created. Regulators continually appealed to professional and business leaders within medicine and pharmacy for numerically based rubrics. Manufacturers supported a legally mandated system of drug therapy because it increased sales and reduced the expense of direct consumer advertising.

In the next chapter, correspondence between federal officials in the Bureau of Chemistry (and its successor, the Food and Drug Administration) and leaders in the United States Pharmacopoeial Convention and National Formulary revision committees presents a negotiated reality regarding the enforceable definitions and standards between pharmaceutical producers. The resolution of this tension, culminated in the Copeland Bill (the federal Food, Drug, and Cosmetic Act of 1938), made the federal government the arbiter of both pharmacopoeial scope and rational therapeutics.

Notes

1.   Brandt, 1987.
2.   This correspondence is in the Robert P. Fischelis papers at the Wisconsin Historical Society, Madison, Wisconsin.

3.   Sonnedecker and Urdang, 1953: 741-760.
4.   Stewart, 1903: 463-466.
5.   Wilbert, 1913: 547.
6.   Stewart, 1917: 9-11, and 1917: 47-49.
7.   McGinnis, 1944: 58.
8.   Ibid., 542.
9.   W. D. Bancroft, Memorandum to members of the Division of Chemistry and Chemical Technology, National Research Council, 30 July 1919, National Archives and Records Administration (hereafter known as NARA), Record Group 88 (hereafter known as RG88), General correspondence—1919-1938 (hereafter known as GC), 1919 decimal file 045.3.
10.   Kebler, 1912: 1165.
11.   Kondratas, 1982: 8-27.
12.   Wilbert, 1904: 150-153.
13.   "Report of a joint committee of the Philadelphia County Medical Society and the Philadelphia College of Pharmacy, relative to physicians' prescriptions" (1852), *New York Journal of Pharmacy* 1: 52-58, found in American Institute of the History of Pharmacy Reference Files, Cowen Collection, especially p. 57 in reference to the apothecary.
14.   Hunt, 1877: 1075-1081, AIHP Cowen Reference Files.
15.   Ibid., 1077.
16.   England, 1908: 602-605.
17.   Cummings, 1929: 13-14.
18.   Wood, 1929: 237-243.
19.   LaWall, 1929: 244-252.
20.   Janssen, 1981: 28-36.
21.   Cummings, 1929: 47-48.
22.   Brandt, 1987: 42.
23.   Quackery in relation to syphilis and gonorrhea in Chicago (1931), American Social Hygiene Association papers (hereafter known as ASHA), Box 99, Folder 3, p. 2.
24.   Anon., 1926, 7(9): 292.
25.   Anon., 1926, 7(1): 37-40.
26.   "Quackery in relation to syphilis and gonorrhea in Chicago" (1931), ASHA, Box 99, Folder 3, p.1.
27.   Ibid., 7, ASHA, Box 99, Folder 3.
28.   Ibid., 18, ASHA, Box 99, Folder 3.
29.   Ibid., 28, ASHA, Box 99, Folder 3.
30.   Ibid., 32, ASHA, Box 99, Folder 3.
31.   Ibid., 5, ASHA, Box 99, Folder 3.
32.   Ibid., 15, ASHA, Box 99, Folder 3.
33.   "Drugstores in relation to venereal disease in Chicago," (1931), p. 12, ASHA, Box 99, Folder 6.
34.   Ibid., 13, ASHA, Box 99, Folder 6.
35.   Ibid., 1, ASHA, Box 99, Folder 6.
36.   Ibid., 3-4, ASHA, Box 99, Folder 6.
37.   "IN RE: Q-1A Health Institute (18 November 1930), p. 1, ASHA, Box 97, Folder 4.
38.   "The medical aspects of social hygiene in Kansas City, Missouri," Section 708—Persons afflicted to be furnished with circular (April 1935), p. 140, ASHA, Box 100, Folder 1.
39.   Ibid., Section 707: Change to physician to be reported, p. 141, ASHA, Box 100, Folder 1.

40. Ibid., Section 712: Powers and duties of Director of Health, p. 146, ASHA, Box 100, Folder 1.
41. Ibid., Section 717: Druggists to keep records of sales for drugs for treatment of— Druggists not to prescribe treatment for—not to compound drugs, etc., p. 148, ASHA, Box 100, Folder 1.
42. No occupation with a connection to medicine's past was left out of control. See Section 981: Regulation of barber shops, barber schools, and barber colleges— inspection—fees and permits—penalty, Ibid., 153, ASHA, Box 100, Folder 1.
43. Ibid., 137, ASHA, Box 100, Folder 1.
44. Ibid., 132-34, ASHA, Box 100, Folder 1.
45. Ibid., 130, ASHA, Box 100, Folder 1.
46. "Drugstores in relation to the venereal diseases in New Orleans," Chapter XXIII, Article 441, Subdivision c (1931), p. 109, ASHA, Box 99, Folder 8.
47. Ibid., 105, ASHA, Box 99, Folder 8.
48. Ibid., 110a, ASHA, Box 99, Folder 8.
49. "A survey of practicing physicians and druggists in East Harlem, New York" (1926), pp. 13, ASHA, Box 100, Folder 12.
50. Beal, 1903: 478-483. See Beal, 1915: 101-107.
51. Brandt, 1987:122-160.
52. Federal action against Massengill, the maker of "Elixir Sulfanilamide," was due to labeling violations involving the diluent, not the drug. The product was not an elixir because it did not contain ethanol as prescribed by the USP. See Young, 1983, "Sulfanilamide and Diethylene Glycol," *Chemistry and Modern Society 6*: 106-125, and Young,1983, "Three Southern Food and Drug Cases," *Journal of Southern History 49* (1): 3-36.
53. Hoover, 1924: 443-444.
54. Wiebe, 1962: 222-223.

5

Negotiating Reality: The Construction of Enforceable Pharmaceutical Standards

Chapter 4, "Dispensing Doctors and Counter-Prescribing Pharmacists," examined conflicting views of pharmaceutical fact and professional propriety surrounding the practices of physicians and pharmacists, with particular reference to treatment of venereal disease. In addition, the professional groups that claimed jurisdiction over the standards of an evolving array of pharmaceutical substances and products were highlighted. The activities and interpretations of an outside observer, the American Social Hygiene Association, were examined with reference to state and federal government efforts to control the incidence and prevalence of venereal diseases.

In this chapter, the evolving arbiter role of the federal government through the Bureau of Chemistry and Food and Drug Administration will be traced. Interaction between government (chemists, pharmacologists, and administrators) and private citizens in professional groups found in the general correspondence files of the Bureau of Chemistry and FDA illustrated the influence of government over the writing of enforceable definitions and standards for pharmaceutical therapies.

Further, this chapter examines those tensions surrounding the construction of enforceable negotiated standards for pharmaceutical production and use between professional groups and the federal government between the Pure Food and Drugs Act of 1906 and the Federal Food, Drug, and Cosmetic Act of 1938, two landmark federal food and drug acts. This "negotiated reality" for enforceable standards centered on the idea of allowable variations for therapeu-

Based on original article that appeared in *Food and Drug Law Journal* 2002: 57(3).

tic substances. Government could not enforce the descriptive "rubrics" of professional formulation despite the elaborate system of local-state-federal cooperation that Harvey Wiley developed, and his successors expanded. Industry and practitioners alike exploited the vagaries of the law by inventing and producing therapeutic substances not covered under existing standards or statutes. Government scientists increasingly pressured pharmacy leaders to revise many aspects of USP and NF, and recommended changes to standards to make enforcement of the 1906 Act more efficient. Over time, this negotiation shifted the content of drug standards from organoleptic qualitative "rubrics" to industrial quantitative monographs.

The notes in the latter portion of the chapter are direct quotations from the general correspondence files of the federal Bureau of Chemistry (BOC) and Food and Drug Administration (FDA) between 1919 and 1936, and illustrate the evolution of ideas related to enforcement of drug laws. The correspondence files are important for several reasons. As Kleinfeld[1] pointed out, the Pure Food and Drugs Act of 1906[2] (1906 Act) was amended only six times until its repeal by the Federal Food, Drug, and Cosmetic Act of 1938[3] (1938 Act). With the exception of Sherley in 1912 (explained later in chapter).[4] its amendments pertained to food law. The Public Health Service ceased publication of the *Abstract of Comments on the USP and NF* in 1922, a function the American Pharmaceutical Association assumed shortly thereafter.[5] Moreover, the federal government did not begin publication of the *Federal Register* until 1936. That only one 1906 Act amendment strictly related to drugs illustrates that the standard bearers and enforcers were in close contact for negotiation and conflict resolution. The correspondence files are an important government repository that contains these day-to-day interactions between interest group leaders to provide a glimpse of how government became the arbiter of pharmaceutical fact.

Between the first and second drug acts, this "negotiated reality" for enforceable standards centered on the idea of allowable variations with respect to their official names, stated tolerances for assay and potency, physical properties, therapeutic dosages, and descriptions for measurement. During this period, BOC and FDA scientists, the United States Pharmacopoeial Convention (USPC), the National Formulary Committee (NF) of the American Pharmaceutical Association (APhA),[6] and the American Medical Association's (AMA)

Council on Pharmacy and Chemistry (CPC)[7] negotiated material, scientific, and enforcement issues of pharmacopoeial scope and rational therapeutics that constituted a social construction of pharmaceutical fact.[8]

The New Chemistry

Many domestic manufacturers began to exploit the discoveries of German laboratory science after the First World War.[9] Under authority of the Trading with the Enemy Act,[10] the Federal Trade Commission (FTC) granted licenses to various leading manufacturers and coastal states for the preparation of synthetic drugs under German patents. The Dermatological Research Laboratories, Takamine Laboratories, H. A. Metz Laboratories, and Diarsenol Company as well as the New York and Massachusetts State Departments of Health were authorized to manufacture arsphenamine and neo-arsphenamine for treatment of venereal diseases. The production of procaine, a local anesthetic, was licensed to Metz, Rector Chemical Co., Abbott Laboratories, and Calco Chemical Co. Barbital (a sedative) and phenyl cinchoninic acid (used in gout), among others received special attention from the National Research Council because these drugs lacked domestic pharmacopoeial standards.

The statutory basis of domestic pharmaceutical standards in the 1906 Act, the United States Pharmacopoeia (USP) did not prescribe any standard for many drugs and therapies of foreign origin. Although used as the basis of enforcement in some states, the pharmacopoeias of other countries were not legally recognized by the federal government. Because of this urgency, the Committee on Synthetic Drugs of the National Research Council advised FTC on "securing manufacturers of important synthetic drugs."[11]

Coal tar was the crude material source for many of these synthetic and natural therapies, including phenol. During World War I, inventor Thomas Edison had taken on the research and production challenges presented by mass manufacture of phenol, or carbolic acid.[12] The war had caused a phenol shortage in America. He asserted in 1915 that his phenol was of higher quality than that required by the USP.[13] "It's better than the Pharmacopoeia calls for—almost like a pure phenol." Phenol became the building block of the new chemistry of the 1920s and 1930s in the United States. Products such as arsphenamine, neoarsphenamine, and acriflavine for venereal diseases, aspirin and phenacetin for pain relief, and barbiturates for insomnia were derived from the phenolic extraction of coal tar. One observer commented, "America did not have these organic chemicals industries before the War."[14]

Industrial mass production of organic pharmaceuticals created tensions between pharmacists, physician, and manufacturers over the distribution and access to those products and the profit derived from their sale. Moreover, standards for industrial production became as closely guarded as the formulations of patent medicines. Pharmacists were thought to often duplicate and sell remedies of their own making once the method of production and formula were known.

The Difficulties of Enforcing the "Rubrics"

Columbia-trained physician Carl L. Alsberg became chief chemist of the BOC after the 1912 retirement of physician-attorney Harvey W. Wiley, BOC's first chief chemist. Alsberg's leadership was characterized by his enforcement of the Sherley amendments to the 1906 Act as well as his interests in "managing" drug trading.[15] The Sherley amendments addressed the perceived lack of enforcement of fraud related to therapeutic claims.[16] Sherley was a Congressional response to a Supreme Court ruling (*United States v. Johnson*)[17] that misbranding provisions of the 1906 Act did not pertain to curative statements. Alsberg directed BOC enforcement primarily at spurious therapeutic and cure claims in product labeling.[18]

As director of Regulatory Work and FDA's first commissioner in 1927, attorney Walter Campbell orchestrated massive administrative reorganization, and led BOC out of the Department of Agriculture.[19] By the end of his tenure, he transformed BOC into FDA under the Federal Security Agency. His career spanned five Republican and two Democratic administrations. Campbell often made very clear to professional leaders, such as E. Fullerton Cook of USPC and Edmund N. Gathercoal of NF, the professions' statutory responsibilities for providing official standards.[20] As the general correspondence files illustrate, BOC encountered problems with their enforcement of largely descriptive rubrics for drug standards. The "rubrics" contained compounding information and organoleptic-based quality standards for extemporaneous preparation. Organoleptic standards are based on sensory perception—how a material looks, feels, smells, and tastes. While BOC often changed its position relative to its involvement in and with standards-setting groups, Campbell was consistent with Wiley's position that government ought to comment about the usefulness of the official compendia.[21] "If the bureau of chemistry cannot have anything to say in regard to standards of analysis and purity which it is called upon to use, times must have gone sadly wrong."[22]

As Anderson and Higby noted, both industry and government played increasingly important roles in USP standards in the 1920s that later led to USPC's admission of proprietary products as official articles.[23] Regulators and industrialists had issues with USP's "professional" standards. Moreover, BOC was not the only federal bureau that encountered enforcement difficulties. The Internal Revenue Bureau documented its problems with alcoholic extract of Jamaica ginger, a popular beverage despite its pungent taste, and a common source of beverage alcohol during Prohibition.[24] As the Internal Revenue Commissioner Donald Roper wrote to BOC Division of Drug's chief Lyman Kebler,[25] the written analytical methods of the BOC did not allow its regulation as a beverage or medicine because it did not specify alcoholic content. While the extraction was to contain at least 20 percent ginger,

> An alcoholic solution of ginger is not a flavoring extract but its use is either a beverage or a medicine…. We are having considerable trouble getting the trade to understand that we intend to insist on a USP alcoholic extract of Jamaica Ginger made absolutely in accordance with the process of the USP…. I hate to criticize anything coming out of the Bureau of Chemistry but to my mind this No. 8 is ridiculous in that instead of following a standard it gives analytical results by which a "fake'" product would be passed by the chemists for the real thing.[26]

Internal Revenue insisted on a product made in accordance with its use as a flavoring agent for food. Otherwise, agents would handle it as "a beverage or a medicine."

As early as 1918, Alsberg requested and received an appropriation from the U.S. Congress for the establishment of reference standards for digitalis, strophanthus, squills, pituitary hormone, ergot, epinephrine, and cannabis. Locating pure references for physiological assay would be a difficult task, as pharmacist-physician R. A. Hatcher of AMA's Council on Pharmacy and Chemistry noted to E. W. Schwartze, Pharmacologist-in-charge of BOC's Laboratory of Pharmacology.

> I believe that there is no pure ouabain [digitalis glycoside] for sale in the United States at present…. I can spare a small amount for scientific research…. Mine is the crystalline product made by Merck…it contains traces of insoluble matter.[27]

The tone of writing standards was a concern to physicians involved in CPC's influential annual commercial compendium, *New and Nonofficial Remedies.* Physician-pharmacologist Julius Steiglitz of CPC had "objected to the pharmacopoeial style" change from the subjunctive to imperative mood. William A. Puckner, Phar.D., the nearly blind secretary of AMA's CPC and its director of the Committee on Chemistry, sought Alsberg's opinion about making *NNR* conform to the new style requirements. Steiglitz's objection may have indicated that he did not want the increasingly obligatory nature for standards in the official pharmacopoeias applied to the choice of therapeutic agents. While Alsberg assigned little importance to the matter, drug compounding directions for pharmacists were in the imperative mood. The tests for identity and purity "were not obligatory," and when "materia medica and preparations" were merged, the style changed to the imperative mood.[28]

Tensions between pharmacists and physicians prompted many pharmacy leaders, like professors Wortley Rudd and Henry Kraemer, to seek a more active standards-setting role from the BOC. As chairman of APhA's section on education and legislation, Rudd invited Alsberg to attend a preliminary pharmacopoeial meeting in early 1919 because

> The contemplated program may cover all the interests having to do directly with USP standards, I am asking that your department be represented at the A.Ph.A. meeting [to participate] in the discussion on Pharmacopoeial Revision.[29]

Alsberg, however, believed it would be inappropriate for the executive branch to become involved in what he thought were essentially legislative matters of law. He would agree to send a representative to speak for the Bureau regarding the administration of law "rather than for the purpose of imposing the ideas of the Bureau on the Association."[30]

As a founding member of the AMA's Council on Pharmacy and Chemistry,[31] Professor Kraemer was more pointed with Alsberg about the evolving conflict surrounding pharmacopoeial scope and rational therapeutics, and the need for a government pharmacopoeia.

> I have felt that as a basic principle we should have in mind that the list of articles to be included [in USP] should be prepared by physicians of the United States and the standards should be worked out by the pharmacists.... This antagonism is growing stronger and I anticipate a strong movement on the part of pharmacists to thwart medical activity...this may be the time to provide for a book that could be used to interpret the Food and Drugs Act and I do not see why the same organization could not be continued, making for the wisest cooperation in the preparation of a work which will safeguard public health and be in the interests of legitimate business...a Government Pharmacopoeia is logical and almost necessary.[32]

Alsberg was concerned that USP standards were not responsive to government or industry. Evidence of the increasing government and corporate influence on standards was Alsberg's idea to create a section of the USP called "Drug Markets." This "special committee," as Cook called it, would be made up of representatives from manufacturing and wholesaling companies, university professors, and federal officials from the BOC and USPHS Hygienic Laboratory. The purpose of the group was to pool knowledge of "firms and government departments that have had experience with the buying of drugs on a large scale."[33] Alsberg's proposed committee embraced the scope of drug "trade" interests.

Allowable Variation

With the federal government responsible for providing reference standards for physiological assay to manufacturers, internal conflicts developed over descriptive rubrics for the determination of potency. E. W. Schwartze advised incoming pharmacologist G. W. Hoover about how the "description of tests in the old pharmacopoeia lacks the precision which chemists desire, as well as confession of the biological inaccuracies." The specific problem, "the method of reasoning by which we deduce the potency" for assaying tincture of digitalis was highlighted:

0.0045 cc. per gram [of frog]—kills no frogs in 1 hr or only a few of a large number.

0.00475 cc. "   " — impracticable to try.

0.005 cc.   "   " — kills about half

0.00525 cc. "   " — impracticable to try.

0.0055 cc. "   " — kills about all.[34]

The method for standardizing the assays did not state allowable variation, and "the biological inaccuracies are likely to constitute the cloak behind which some will try to hide." The government's standard for potency must account for variation in line with that found in the experience of "commercial houses."[35] At that time, academic discussions provided the regulatory staff with no legal way of interpreting the actual data because for legal purposes the potency of a preparation was not stated to vary on different animals.

The USP contained other "errors" related to nomenclature and the omission of salt forms of many products. Henry Fuller of the Industrial Research Laboratories commented to Lyman Kebler that these errors allowed the introduction of "inferior medicinal agents." Fuller wrote, "It seems to me as if the Committee is at fault in admitting only the alkaloids themselves. The salts are the substances with which the doctor and pharmacist have to deal..." Testing procedures should also include those that allowed differential identification between chemically similar substances, like aethylmorphine hydrochloride and codeine.[36]

Within the same time period as the reference standards program, the Federal Specifications Board (FSB) was created in 1921.[37] FSB's purpose was to derive uniform federal standards for determining the award of contracts to producers that supplied various goods for government purchase. Several members of the USPC "felt some concern" (as had Harvey W. Wiley with the creation of the Bureau of Standards in 1901) that standards proposed by the American Engineering Standards Committee for medicinal and edible oils would encroach on USP's statutory authority. The Committee-proposed specifications included expressed oil of almond, castor oil, cod liver oil, and croton oil. Writing to Walter Campbell, Cook asked, "Why is this Committee working on standards for USP preparations?"[38] Campbell replied that the purpose of the Board was to "unify Government specifications" and "in no way do they interfere with the revision of the Pharmacopoeia." To the government, USP standards for cottonseed and olive oils were not adequate for establishing its purchasing requirements.

Any specification adopted by the Federal Specifications Board may be revised at any time circumstances warrant a change, consequently whenever your Revision Committee improves any of the USP specifications for these oils, the Government is in a position to consider such changes at once.[39]

Cook concluded, "There of course should not be two organizations working at cross-purposes on these standards."[40]

As chairman of the Association of Official Agricultural Chemists (AOAC)[41] Pharmacopoeial Committee, Lyman Kebler questioned Cook as to the determination of percentage and boiling point variation for creosol, a coal tar derivative.[42] Kebler wrote, "The standard reads 'Not less than 90 per cent by volume of Creosol distills between 195 and 205 degrees C.'" He seemed to challenge Cook as to whether this range constituted a standard at all. Cook referred to a USP member (probably USPC Board of Trustees Chairman James Hartley Beal's son, Mellon Institute director of research George Denton Beal) "who was thoroughly familiar with the work being done in the American Society for Testing Materials." Further, Cook indicated that the boiling point range details "as set forth on page 598 USP IX, were quite sufficiently detailed to give satisfactory results."[43] The Bureau believed, Kebler held, that the range for distillation could be more exact as evidenced by a technical paper from the Bureau of Mines for the distillation of gasoline. These technical standards were important because "you, of course, realize that all standards and methods in the Pharmacopoeia possess more or less of a legal status and therefore the utmost care should be used to avoid the possibility of mistakes creeping into the work of analysts."[44]

Further communication from Kebler to Cook indicated the topical nature of USP standards as they affected, and fell short of, the enforcement of law in other bureaus.

> The other day while discussing the olive oil soap standard for the Pharmacopoeia with Mr. P. H. Walker of the Bureau of Standards, he expressed himself rather vigorously regarding the defective nature of the standard, stating that he thought the committee of revision ought to introduce a worth while standard into the Pharmacopoeia. I told him that some of us at least, thought that the standard was fairly good but that if he had anything that would make for improvement if he would send me same, I would be glad to place it at your disposal. In harmony with this understanding, he sent me a copy each of US Government standard specification No. 26, and US Government Master Specification for milled toilet soap. [45]

Lyman Kebler was educated as a pharmacist and physician, and was experienced in pharmaceutical manufacturing at Smith Kline. Employed by the federal government for twenty-seven years (1902-1929), he joined the Bureau as the first chief of the division of drugs under Harvey Wiley. Kebler always sought harmonious relations with the professions, serving on numerous committees in APhA, AMA, and AOAC, as well as the 1920-1930 Revision Committee of USP. With the change of bureau leadership in 1921 from Alsberg, the physician, to Campbell, the attorney, the nature of Kebler's interactions with the Pharmacopoeia seemed to change as well.[46]

From the Bosom of the Family

Harvey Wiley's death in 1930 seemed to re-stimulate the public call for government action against the perception of corrupt trade practices in food and drugs.[47] Consumers Research, Inc., a private, non-commercial organization, began circulation of the *Consumer Research General Bulletin* in 1931. Its technical director, F. J. Schlink, directed the organization's anti-corruption campaign against both government and business. The bulletin's inaugural issue in September 1931 also attacked the AMA and *Good Housekeeping* magazine over approving a product called Vapex, a popular household remedy, which contained unlabeled ethanol.[48] The lead article was entitled, "The Consumer and His Protection by the Government." At the 1931 National Association of Retail Grocers' convention, Robert LaFollette, the governor of Wisconsin and perennial presidential candidate, echoed a common progressive theme: "The relation of government and business is nothing less than a corporation of which we are stockholders, and the government at the state capitals are the boards of directors..."[49]

Wiley, Schlink, and LaFollette had one thing in common. Each was devoted to the importance of pure food. They differed, however, as to the level of control exerted by government. Wiley always sided with producers. Schlink advocated only for consumers. LaFollette wanted government modulation of all economic trading between the two sides. Walter Campbell shared Wiley's concern for fairness to producers as well as LaFollette's popular sentiment about fair enforcement by government. To incoming National Formulary (NF) Chairman Edmund Gathercoal, he wrote:

> In previous revisions of the National Formulary monographs for preparations have appeared which presented difficulties to this Administration when attempting under the terms of the Federal Food and Drugs Act to enforce the standards set up.... In this division bulletins will be subject to review by all who are interested in the Drug Control work of this Department...[and] made wholly in the spirit of cooperation with your Committee...[50]

At the time, the NF was a compendium of pharmaceutical formulas in common use by pharmacists. Its purpose was to provide instructions for uniform extemporaneous compounding as an alternative to propriety medicines. With the USP, NF provided pharmaceutical standards for the 1906 Act even though the NF's original conception was not to provide standards. As such, Campbell held that the professionals should provide the government with accurate, scientifically current standards, "free from ambiguity and that they may be kept abreast of scientific developments. We hope your organization will succeed ...in adopting this policy."[51]

J. J. Durrett, Chief of Drug Control, wrote to Henry V. Arny,[52] Dean of Columbia College of Pharmacy and NF member, regarding the lack of anti-bacterial properties of *Liquor Antisepticus*, a mouthwash formulation. Government bacteriologists had devised a methodology for testing its properties, and found that the alcohol content of *Liquor Antisepticus* was not sufficient for killing a wide variety of bacteria. They said that the official formula should be changed, perhaps to *Liquor Aromaticus*, or its name modified to describe its true properties. Durrett even questioned the necessity for a mouthwash to have antiseptic characteristics.

> We have reached the conclusion that the product prepared according to the official formula for *Liquor Antisepticus* is so near the borderline when tested according to the procedure we have adopted for use in cases arising under the provisions of the law, that any slight variation in its composition, as for example in the content of alcohol or any slight variation in the resistance of the organism used for testing, may result in either a positive or a negative bacteriologic finding…. If the Committee so desires, we will carry out a suitable investigation and make recommendations regarding the modification of the formula. If on the other hand the Committee decides to retain the present formula and changes the title from *Liquor Antisepticus* to *Liquor Aromaticus*, as has been suggested, it is of course immaterial whether or not the product possesses antiseptic properties. In fact, I may say that so far as the Administration is concerned we see no particular reason why gargles and mouthwashes should be antiseptic. Perhaps if the product contains 31% it would be consistently found antiseptic, whereas if it contains only 25% it would probably be consistently nonantiseptic.[53]

F. J. Cullen, who became chief of drug control on Durrett's promotion to Division of Drugs Chief, notified Gathercoal that Dr. Durrett was expressing not only his opinion, but also that of the entire staff at the Bureau who deal with the testing of products such as *Liquor Antisepticus*. The change in alcoholic content was merely a "suggestion as to a possible solution to the problem."

> Apparently, the members of your committee have gained the impression that a slight increase in alcohol content will make the product definitely antiseptic… Any proposed formula should, of course, be submitted to actual bacteriological tests before it is adopted.[54]

Gathercoal apologized for members of the Committee who he said were used to expressing themselves not publicly, but "from the bosom of the family." The Committee, however, did not "wish to stand on any false or misleading premise" regarding the article's title or composition.

> We would like very much to preserve the present title of *Liquor Antisepticus*…[and] will give very serious consideration to strengthening of the antiseptic powers of the preparation and if we cannot do this we will change the name.[55]

Together, Durrett, Cullen, and Senior Chemist A. G. Murray constituted FDA's resolve to quantify descriptive rubrics.[56] They reviewed and commented on every aspect of any product or its stated therapeutic use, and recommended omission of products without scientific merit from future editions. Conditions for use should be clearly specified.[57] If the product's name did not accurately describe its action, FDA suggested changes to it or its constituents. When purer forms became available, government scientists advised both Cook and Gathercoal to adjust official listings to account for improved ingredients. But, while a new phenol compound mixture might be useful to the trade,[58] "ordinary ether is entirely satisfactory for use as a reagent." [59]

Expression of dosages in either official compendium were desired by physicians, but often omitted by pharmacists because of the therapeutic nature of posology. But, because of its widespread use and potential toxicity, Cullen questioned the dosage recommendation for caffeine, and suggested that it include some qualifying statement for use.

> Dosage for caffeine...recommended...would probably represent an average dose where used as an emergency stimulant. We believe such a dose too large to be used as an average dose in combination with other drugs as, for example, there are on the market numerous proprietary remedies recommended for the treatment of headaches, colds and similar conditions which contain one grain or more of caffeine in addition to certain other ingredients such as aspirin, acetanilid, etc. The inclusion of this large dosage in the Pharmacopoeia unqualified is likely to result in the manufacturers' of medicinal preparations including this dose of caffeine in their proprietary mixtures, which may prove dangerous to many individuals.[60]

Cook included Cullen's suggestions with other comments recently issued in the *USP Circular*, a members-only newsletter.[61]

This running commentary between government officials and professional leaders became especially apparent when the federal government transferred responsibility for reference standards to the USP.[62] Due to a change in policy, in June 1932, Campbell informed Cook that Food and Drug was to "...discontinue the distribution of standards for the various bioassay drugs..." for industry, and inquired whether the USP could take over this function.[63] Cullen supplied Cook with an exact accounting of the amount of requests from industry during the preceding year so that USP could gauge demand for samples.

> From July 1, 1930 to June 30, 1931, we have sent out the following amounts of official standard preparations. Cannabis, 30 ampuls; Epinephrine, 20 ampuls; Ergot, 280 ampuls; Pituitary, powdered posterior lobe, 25 ampuls; Ouabain, 28 ampuls.[64]

Cook replied to Murray, "We are endeavoring to work out a plan by which the Pharmacopoeia can efficiently assume this responsibility..."[65]

Corrosive Sublimate, USP (mercuric bichloride tablets), a topical anti-syphllitic, tested the limits of government intervention and responsibility. Most tablets of the time were white in color. Many companies were selling unofficial bichloride tablets that did not conform to USP-specified shape or blue color. A personal friend of E. Fullerton Cook died of an accidental poisoning, mistaking poisonous bichloride tablets for aspirin.[66] Paul Dunbar, FDA assistant chief, wrote to Cullen and Murray, asking if they thought FDA could insist on the shape and color, and thereby prosecute based on adulteration or misbranding. "Does the solution hold that we can insist on the shape and color requirements on p. 407 of USP?"[67] Larrick suggested that the case should be developed on "the identical shipment involved in the poisoning." Crawford set out to determine "if the possibility exists that the goods [are] still available."[68]

USP rubrics required that corrosive mercuric chloride tablets have an angular shape, not discoid, with the word "POISON" and skull and crossbones embossed on it. The tablets were colored blue, preferably with sodium indigotinisulfonate.[69] In a memo to FDA Eastern District chief, Dunbar expressed the informal opinion of the Solicitor's office. While "no allegation of adulteration" could be substantiated,

> When this product is sold under one of the names listed in the Pharmacopoeia the allegation of misbranding may be established on the ground that the color, at least, and possibly the shape, are factors of identity, and that if corrosive sublimate tablets do not possess the color and shape specified in the Pharmacopoeia they are not identical with the pharmacopoeial article and are therefore not entitled to unqualified pharmacopoeial names.[70]

E. Fullerton Cook warned both the distributor, Whalen Drug, and the producer of the white discoid tablets, John Wyeth & Bros. Further investigation revealed that the tablets were purchased in accordance with Pennsylvania's poison laws. Nevertheless, pharmacists contacted boards of pharmacy to inquire whether federal officials, in California board secretary Zeh's words, "were going to act against the sale of these tablets...especially Berney's," a popular Upjohn product.[71] While not manufactured in FDA's Eastern or Western Districts, "the mercuric chloride tablets on the market are generally not the USP article." "In view of the Eastern District's report on the general conditions found which must have included Central District manufacturers, I believe it would be a waste of time to put any further effort on this project. The Western District has no manufacturers of mercuric bichloride tablets."[72] Cullen felt that the standard could not be adjudicated, and seemed to realize Cook's emphasis and attention to detail in light of his friend's death from accidental poisoning.

> We are somewhat apprehensive about the use of such general terms as "suitable excipi-
> ent," "distinctive color." Who is to decide what excipient is "suitable" and what color is
> "distinctive".... Under such a condition would not a +/- 10% variation be unnecessarily
> large?... It is suggested that in the proposed text the wording be modified to read "not
> less than 0.45 Gm. and not more than 0.55 Gm. of absolute mercuric chloride ($HgCl_2$)."[73]

Cook indicated to Cullen, "Before any bichloride text is adopted
I shall ask you to review the proposals."[74]

Standards for the moisture content of hygroscopic drugs, geo-
graphic and climatic variation, dosages, and optical refractometry
continued to be negotiated between the government's chemists and
pharmacologists and USP's Cook. Why specify two separate monographs for "heavy" and "light" mineral oil, Cook asked Cullen, when
"any oil falling within the ranges named, might be properly call 'Liquid Petrolatum'."[75] Would it make any practical difference?

Cullen knew that the physical differences between various grades
of mineral oil, expressed in one standard, would not allow for efficient regulation.

> We are aware that a precedent for including two different articles in one monograph
> exists in the case of liquid petrolatum. It would seem, however, that it would be much
> better to describe such articles in two separate monographs...[76]

The USP, Cullen maintained, should be applicable in a variety of
climatic conditions, "in the tropics as well as Alaska."[77] Allowable
variations should be written into standards, Cook agreed, and "the
present Pharmacopoeia on Page 410 permits this [variation] for
Unguentum and also on Page 103 for Ceratum."[78]

Murray indicated to Cook that a variation in temperature altered the
results of tests for optical rotation and refractive index. "Since constant
temperature rooms for optical work are ordinarily maintained at 20
degrees C, it is suggested that consideration be given to the advisability
of adopting 20 degrees C as a standard temperature for polarimetric
work."[79] Cook agreed, and would pose the question to USP experts. "A
conference on chemical questions will be held in a few weeks and I
shall at that time ask the group to consider all of your proposals."[80]

Allowable variation was always a moving target. The names of
products could not vary: There was only one official name for each
preparation. If, however, the variation aided enforcement of law and
mass production, standards were often lowered or changed to give
"some leniency to the general statement in the Pharmacopoeia."[81] In
the case of tinctures, the assumed 10 percent standard was not written into the monographs, and

While the statement "10 gm. of standard drug to 100 cc of tincture" was the original idea, and is still intended in a general way to be the standard for tinctures, the variation in content of active principle in assayed drugs is so great that sometimes the tincture does not even approximate the composition mentioned. In any event, the monographs themselves do not specify such a standard.[82]

As Murray pointed out to Cook,

Numerous illustrations taken from preparations in the Pharmacopoeia and National Formulary might be cited to illustrate the difficulty arising from indefinite standards for drugs in determining whether or not preparations of them have been properly manufactured. One particular outstanding example is emetine hydrochloride, which is described as containing "variable amounts of water of crystallization" and which, upon drying to constant weight, "loses not more than 10% of water." The definition of this article, we have no doubt, could easily be made reasonably definite by prescribing a minimum as well as a maximum loss upon drying. It is our understanding that, as a matter of fact, the salt in commerce is of reasonably uniform composition.[83]

The purity of solid samples was often tested by determining a substance's melting point. Several samples of pilocarpine FDA examined melted at temperatures in excess of the official standard. Murray recommended to Cook that…"helpful information as to the melting point of this drug can doubtless be supplied by the manufacturers of it."[84]

Murray also recommended to Cook how to denote mass. "…Where the expression '0.001 Gm.' occurs. '1 Mg.' would seem to us preferable."[85] Always eager to clarify any aspect of the Pharmacopoeia, Cook agreed that "…when a fraction of a gram is so small that it is better understood if it is expressed in milligrams, that should be the course followed in the Pharmacopoeia."[86] Cook's respect for Murray's insightful and critical review of the *Circulars* was clearly evident.[87]

Because USP was now responsible for reference standards, Murray, Cullen, and Durrett often gave Cook and Gathercoal the benefit of their experience in preparations of bioassays. In developing the reference standard for cod liver oil, one of USP's new vitamin references, Murray commented that

The determination of unsaponifiable matter in cod liver oil is faulty…Mr. George S. Jamisson of the Bureau of Chemistry and Soils, who is the author of the modification of the Kerr-Sorber method as it appears in the AOAC book, assures me that the method is entirely reliable for cod liver oil. I feel that no mistake would be made by the Revision Committee in adopting either the modified Kerr-Sorber method or the modified USP method.[88]

It has been the practice of this Administration in determining alcohol to provide that the distillate shall contain no more than 25%, and preferably from 15% to 20%, of alcohol. We do not know that the proposed procedure which permits the distillate to contain up to 30% is liable to yield too low results. If actual data on this subject are not available, it is suggested that they be obtained before so high a percentage of alcohol in the distillate is provided for.... In the last paragraph but one, on page 120, second line, following the word "dilute," if the words "a measured volume of" were inserted, misunderstanding might be avoided.[89]

Allowable variation was encouraged where it could be stated in numeric units. Encountered by both Cook and Gathercoal, descriptive variation, such as "variable amounts of water of crystallization," "suitable excipients," and "distinctive color" were too indefinite because "the finished product cannot be held to a definite requirement as to composition."[90] But, as Cook responded earlier, a purity rubric and constant weight basis is impracticable because "...the hygroscopic or deliquescent character of chemicals is uncontrollable, and too rigid a limitation might do injustice."[91] Cullen conceded that individual pharmacists would have difficulty meeting this requirement, but reiterated that consumers deserved a better standard.[92]

It is not practicable for the pharmacist to determine from time to time the degree of efflorescence of his stock of quinine sulphate. I dare say that the ordinary practice is to weigh the material from the stock bottle in the prescribed amount by a physician regardless of any efflorescence. This does not make much of a problem for the pharmaceutical manufacturer who is compounding preparations on a large scale and who can maintain chemical control over the finished preparation... Our conviction grows that it would be in the interest of consumers generally to have described in the Pharmacopoeia a quinine sulphate of more stable composition than that not official.[93]

Cook recognized that products prepared by pharmacists and those from manufacturers were of different composition. "I appreciate your calling our attention to the available character of the commercial product [quinine sulphate and quinidine sulphate] and hope that we can make a more satisfactory standard."[94]

The quality of ergot preparations emerged as a concern to regulators because industrial modifications did not conform to NF standards for the fluidextract. In fact, Lilly's " extract" was "about four times the strength of Standard Fluidextract of Ergot [which] is now being marketed."[95] Cullen implored Gathercoal to reveal the name of the Lilly research head so that an official monograph might be developed in accordance with the new strength. "The conversation with Mr. Bibbins [chief pharmacist at Lilly] was a private one," Gathercoal maintained, "and I think that it would be well not to publish his name nor that of his firm until we have permission to do so."[96] To Cullen, the problem was labeling. [97]

> Very likely Eli Lilly & Co. makes no statement on the label of this preparation [Extract of Ergot] regarding its assay strength because such statements are not made by other manufacturers. The statement was made to me by the head of their research department with the understanding that I should not publish it.[98]

Despite Gathercoal's request for privacy, Cullen instructed senior pharmacologist William T. McClosky to contact Bibbins regarding the method Lilly used to produce the extraction. He wrote to Bibbins, "If consistent with your firm's policy I should appreciate direct information as to the facts."[99] While Bibbins indicated the general method of preparation in "acid-aqueous menstrum" that distinguished it from competitors, he did not specify the exact finishing process.

> Lilly's Powdered Extract Ergot is made by a special process which includes extraction of the drug in an acid-aqueous menstrum and then a powdered extract is finished by a process developed in the Lilly Laboratories, which for obvious reasons we would not care to divulge. The powdered extract is then tested by the USP physiological assay method for Ergot, and diluted to standard strength with powdered ergot. One gram powdered extract equals four grams Ergot.[100]

He assured McClosky that the resultant powder was assayed in accordance with USP standards for ergot, and "one gram powdered extract equals four grams Ergot." Cullen again wrote to Gathercoal that the next NF should contain this extract if its potency could be determined and maintained in production.

> We see no reason why a powdered extract of ergot should not be placed in the National Formulary, Sixth edition, provided such extract will be of a definite potency, and an assay method adopted which will be capable of determining such potency.[101]

The Legal Thinking of Walter Campbell

Of the over 15,000 legal opinions filed by the Solicitor's office between 1910 and 1937, less than fifty concerned BOC and FDA.[102] Walter Campbell had wide administrative responsibilities as director of Regulatory Work, but did not frequently request the written opinion of the Department of Agriculture's solicitor. When he did solicit opinion provides insight into his legal thinking regarding the federal role in interstate commerce. Regulation of pharmaceutical commerce required less comment from the solicitor because the federal government had deferred standards-setting for pharmaceuticals to professional groups of physicians and pharmacists.

Campbell's leadership of federal enforcement of the 1906 Act was typified by thorough legal justification for taking any action.[103] He was a career agent who, by the 1930s, had become increasingly impatient with the medical and pharmaceutical professions whose standards his agency was charged to police. His position was that any batch of any product must not vary from any USP definition. Otherwise, the product would be considered misbranded. For example, under his administration, ointments and cerates (wax- or resin-containing preparations) sold under official names were regarded as legal only if they conformed strictly to the specifications given in the individual monographs. "No specified ingredient may be omitted and no unspecified material may be used."[104]

An officially recognized name described a genuine article that could be measured quantitatively. However, even the official names of many articles in the USP and NF posed regulatory problems because they did not characterize enforceable compositions.[105] Cullen told Gathercoal that "Hive syrup" should be removed from the NF because the name denoted the "use of therapeutically significant designations." [106] Use of the word "compound" to describe mixtures of crude ingredients was misleading, and "this would be in harmony with Mr. Campbell's recommendation concerning 'compounds' as embodied in his letter of July 21, 1933…"[107]

> I suppose what is meant [by dilute sulphuric acid] is something like "1 per cent sulphuric acid"…an official preparation and the term should preferably not be used in the National Formulary or United States Pharmacopoeia unless the official article is intended.[108]

Industry and government continued to work out the determination and refinement of standards for commercially available substances.[109] R. T. Balch of carbohydrate division of the Bureau of Chemistry and Soils validated the revision of standards for sugars prepared by George Denton Beal at the Mellon Institute.[110]

Because of the widespread misuse of official names and the movement in many states for enactment of their own drug laws, Campbell asked Gathercoal to comment on a trade notice being prepared by the Administration. "The issuance of USP XI and NF VI [in 1936] are naturally bringing considerable correspondence to the Administration in connection with the changes which have been made." This notice would specify, in detail, the exact nature of federal enforcement for the use of official names.[111] The notice "appears to me to correctly interpret the intention of the Revision Committee." However, Durrett directed Gathercoal to "call upon us [in early October] to discuss problems of this Administration arising by reason of the official status of the National Formulary."[112]

The Negotiation of Quantitative Standards

Government could not enforce the descriptive "rubrics" of professional formulation despite the elaborate system of local-state-federal cooperation that Harvey Wiley developed, and his successors expanded. Industry and practitioners alike exploited the vagaries of the law by inventing and producing therapeutic substances not covered under existing standards or statutes. Government scientists continually negotiated with industry and organization leaders to create and validate quantitative standards based on the results of evolving experimental science. Official standards had to be universally applicable for the purposes of governing trade. Often, vague specifications left regulators in search of other mechanisms, like the Federal Specifications Board and engineering groups, to reconcile the differences between standard and statute.

Industrial production of new synthetic compounds clearly changed the focus of government interaction with the revision committees. Government scientists increasingly pressured Cook and Gathercoal to revise many aspects of USP and NF. They were impatient with the lack of progress in changing the standards' descriptive specifications, especially after the USP assumed from FDA the production and distribution of reference assays. Government chemists, pharmacologists, and bacteriologists recommended variations in standards when it made enforcement of the 1906 Act more efficient. Over time, this negotiation shifted the content of drug standards from organoleptic qualitative "rubrics" to industrial quantitative monographs.

Notes

1. Kleinfeld, 1995: 65-99.
2. Pub. L. 59-384, 34 Stat. 786 (1906).
3. Pub. L. 75-717, 21 U.S.C. 301-392 (1938).
4. 37 Stat. 416 (1912).
5. Anderson and Higby, 1995: 233.
6. The history of the National Formulary is found in Higby, 1989.
7. The interactions between the Council on Pharmacy and Chemistry and the federal government is described in Marks, 1997: 23-41.
8. For the social construction of other aspects of pharmaceutical production and therapy, see D. Dingeslstad et al., 1996: 1829-38.
9. F. M. Phelps, National Research Council, to M. W. Glover, Drug Administration, Bureau of Chemistry, 24 October 1919, Record Group 88 (hereafter known as

RG88), National Archives and Records Administration (hereafter known as NARA), General correspondence—1919-1938 (hereafter known as GC), 1919 decimal file 045.3.

10.   40 Stat. 411 (1917).

11.   Wilder D. Bancroft to members of the Division of Chemistry and Chemical Technology, National Research Council, 30 July 1919, RG88, NARA, GC, 1919 decimal file 045.3.

12.   "Thomas A. Edison on Dye Situation," *Pharmaceutical Era 48* (5): 199-200 (1915).

13.   "Edison Elated over Success in Making Synthetic Phenol," *Pharmaceutical Era 48* (9): 402 (1915).

14.   "Pharmacy and the New Chemistry," *Pharmaceutical Era 55* (2): 41-3 (1922).

15.   The 50th Anniversary Special Issue of the *Food and Drug Law Journal* contains career history of various leaders of the Food and Drug Administration and its predecessors. Much of the series appeared previously in the Food Drug and Cosmetic Law Quarterly and Journal. Alsberg's career is summarized by an eyewitness in F. B. Linton, "Federal Food and Drug Laws—Leaders Who Achieved Their Enactment and Enforcement—Part II," *Food and Drug Law Journal 50*: 21-9 (1995) and "Part III," at 29-37.

16.   37 Stat. 416 (1912).

17.   221 U.S. 488 (1911).

18.   Young, 1967.

19.   Linton, 1995: 49-58.

20.   Both Cook and Gathercoal were Remington Medallists of the American Pharmaceutical Association. For a synopsis of their careers, see Griffenhagen, Blockstein, and Kraigstein 1994: 58-65, 86-94.

21.   Linton, 1995: 9-20.

22.   Joseph. P. Remington, Dr. Wiley's Position, 4 November 1911, RG88, NARA, Records of the United States Pharmacopoeia (USP), Committee of Revision (1910-1940), Box 1, Volume 2.

23.   Anderson and Higby, 1995: 232-3.

24.   Often adulterated to mask the ginger's resin, Jamaica ginger later caused paralysis because of tri-o-cresyl phosphate, a coal tar derivative once used for treating tuberculosis. See Parascandola, 1994: 123-131.

25.   A brief sketch of Kebler's professional life is found in King, 1987: 69-70.

26.   D. Roper to L. F. Kebler, 8 March 1919, GC, 1919 decimal file 500.41.

27.   R. A. Hatcher to E. W. Schwartze, 18 April 1919.

28.   William A. Puckner to Carl L. Alsberg, 4 April 1919; Alsberg to Puckner, 29 April 1919.

29.   Wortley F. Rudd (Professor of Chemistry, Medical College of Virginia) to Carl L. Alsberg, 7 May 1919.

30.   Alsberg to Rudd, 14 May 1919.

31.   Simmons, 1905: 718-721.

32.   H. Kraemer to Alsberg, 27 May 1919.

33.   Alsberg to E. F. Cook, Chairman, Committee of Revision, United States Pharmacopoeial Convention, 15 December 1920; Cook to Alsberg, 20 December 1920.

34.   E. W. Schwartze to G.W. Hoover, 5 January 1923, GC, 1923 decimal file 500.41.

35.   Schwartze to Hoover, 5 January 1923.

36.   H. C. Fuller to L. F. Kebler, 21 January 1922.

37.   Dupree, 1957.

38.   E. F. Cook to W. G. Campbell, 16 May 1923.

39.   Campbell to Cook, 20 June 1923.

40.   Cook to Campbell, 26 June 1923.

41. Harvey W. Wiley (a former Indiana state chemist) created AOAC, now called Association of Official Analytical Chemists. For its contributions to regulatory administration, see Hutt, 1985: 147-151.
42. Kebler to Cook, 8 October 1924.
43. Cook to Kebler, 28 October 1924.
44. Kebler to Cook, 7 November 1924.
45. Kebler to Cook, 18 November 1924.
46. The general correspondence files in RG88 contain no letters related to standards between the period 1925 and 1929.
47. R. Millard, "Wiley's Fight for Honesty Not Yet Won," 6 July 1930, RG88, NARA, General Records of the FDA and its predecessors; Records relating to the laxness of enforcement, Box 1, Book 1.
48. F. J. Schlink, "The Consumer and His Protection by the Government," RG88, NARA, General Records of the FDA and its predecessors; Records relating to the laxness of enforcement, Box 1, Book 1. Schlink, "Government Bureaus for Private Profit," Box 1, Book 1. P. B. Dunbar, Memorandum to be attached to September, 1931 Consumers' Research General Bulletin, 13 October 1931.
49. R. A. LaFollette, "Equality of Opportunity," RG88, NARA, Articles and speeches, 1916-1964.
50. W. G. Campbell to E. N. Gathercoal, 4 August 1930, 1930 decimal file 500.42.
51. J. J. Durrett to E. F. Kelly, 21 June 1931, 1931 decimal file 500.42.
52. See Griffenhagen, Blockstein, and Kraigstein, 1994: 20-25.
53. J. J. Durrett to H. V. Arny, 5 August 1931.
54. F. J. Cullen to E. N. Gathercoal, 7 October 1931.
55. Gathercoal to Cullen, 19 October 1931, RG88.
56. Durrett to Gathercoal, 13 July 1931. "Because the method of preparation specified by the NF 5th edition for Aqueous Extract of Ergot has been found to result in a product which is practically devoid of specific ergot alkaloids, regardless of the alkaloid content of the parent drug, it is recommended that this or any other preparation not containing significant and defined amounts of specific ergot alkaloidal activity be omitted from succeeding editions." Cullen to Gathercoal, 10 November 1933. "Under coal tar it is provided that the article leaves 'not more than 2 per cent of ash.' Orthocreosol obtained from coal tar which yields more than 2 per cent of ash technically must be regarded as adulterated..." Cullen to Gathercoal, 29 November 1933. "'...Dilute sulphruic acid' I suppose what is meant is something like '1 per cent sulphuric acid.' Dilute sulphuric acid, however, is an official preparation and the term should preferably not be used in the National Formulary or United States Pharmacopoeia unless the official article is intended." Cullen to Gathercoal, 20 December 1933, "'Compound' in some of the National Formulary monographs where it may readily conceal real information about the composition of the article from anyone not immediately familiar with the formulas of the products... 'Compound Fluidextract of Trifolium' does not adequately convey an impression regarding its actual composition."
57. J. J. Durrett to H. V. Arny, 2 July 1931. "Antiseptic powder of the National Formulary is antiseptic when used as a dry powder dressing, but it is not antiseptic when used even in saturated solution. If this article is retained in the National Formulary, in our opinion a statement should be made in the monograph to the effect that the article is antiseptic only when used as a powder and not in solution ..."
58. Durrett to Gathercoal, 14 August 1931. "It has occurred to me that it might be advisable for the National Formulary to recognize a compound solution of phenols manufactured after the general formula of the compound creosol solution but containing the higher boiling point phenols instead of creosol."

59. Murray to Cook, 2 September 1931. "The present Pharmacopoeia recognizes two ethers, one in the monographs, and other (ether, dehydrated) under 'Reagents.' We can see no particular use in having any others specified. The ordinary ether is entirely satisfactory for use as a reagent."

60. Cullen to Cook, 29 October 1932, 1932 decimal file 500.41.

61. Cook to Cullen, 31 October 1932.

62. See Anderson and Higby, 1995, 294-5.

63. W. G. Campbell to E. F. Cook, 3 June 1932.

64. F. J. Cullen to E. F. Cook, 26 September 1932. The correspondence files are replete with requests from manufacturers for bioassays. G. F. Cartland, Upjohn Company to Food and Drug Administration, requesting ergot and pituitary standard samples, 22 June 1932. W. T. McClosky to Upjohn Company, 22 June 1932.

65. Cook to A. G. Murray, 5 October 1932. USP successfully assumed the reference standards program, and expanded its scope by adding vitamins (1932), anti-anemia preparations (1935), endocrinology products (1938), among others. For a discussion of this transfer and subsequent development, see Anderson and Higby, 1995: 294-296.

66. A. E. Lowe to Food and Drug Administration, P. B. Dunbar and C. W. Crawford, 18 April 1932. A personal friend of Dr. Cook's died after mistaking mercuric chloride for aspirin tablets. This letter details the sale of those tablets. "Sale was made as bichloride tablets and the purchaser who was a personal friend of Dr. Cook's was required to state the intended use and sign the poison register...Dr. Cook warned both the Whelan Drug Company and John Wyeth & Bros. as to the general danger connected with the sale of tablets of this type...numerous brands of bichloride tablets on the market that are not strictly USP. Philadelphia also refers to such products as put out by Eli Lilly & Co., H.K. Mulford, etc."

67. P. B. Dunbar, Memorandum to F. J. Cullen and A. G. Murray, 23 February 1932.

68. G. P. Larrick, Memorandum to C.W. Crawford, 22 March 1932; C. W. Crawford, Memorandum to G. P. Larrick, 23 March 1932.

69. E. F. Cook, "USP bichloride tablets," *Oil, Paint, and Drug Reporter*, 15 February 1932.

70. P. B. Dunbar, Memorandum to Eastern District Chief, 19 March 1932; C. W. Crawford, Memorandum to Eastern District Chief, 23 March 1932; D. M. Walsh, Memorandum to Eastern District Chief, 15 April 1932. "Mr. Minshall took up with Mr. Murray the matter of whether this 'Antiseptic Tablet' might be considered in violation because of its round shape, but Mr. Murray stated that they wanted only tablets labeled 'Corrosive Sublimate USP' so that I doubt if we can secure the desired official sample here."

71. L. Zeh to United States Department of Public Health, 29 April 1932, "April Merck report and...Southern California Druggists' Association relative to "Corrosive Sublimate Tablets as now being sold in many states and not conforming to the shape as required by the USP...[board of pharmacy] has the enforcement of the poison law of this state..."; W. S. Frisbie to L. Zeh, Secretary, California Board of Pharmacy, 14 May 1932. "You refer to an article which appeared in the April issue of Merck's sales report stating that there are now being sold in many States 'Corrosive Sublimate Tablets' not conforming to the shape required by the USP." E. O. Eaton to Western District Chief, 19 May 1932, "Today, I telephoned Mr. Louis Zeh, Secretary, California Board of Pharmacy, re Mr. Frisbie's communication of 14 May, last. Our files do not show why Mr. Zeh took up this matter originally. I was requested to interview him by Mr. Norton...we would act by seizure if a violation of our act could be shown; however, from a study of the current pharmaceutical manufacturers' trade catalogs I noted that some were not of the size, color or shape as specified

by USP and some were of different drug strength as well as expicient...I assume the Administration is familiar with Berney's Tablets (Bichloride, large and small—see the Upjohn Catalog), as well as the Wilson Tablet (blue and white) of Parke, Davis & Co. Other manufacturers classify these tablets in similar manner.... This question is so closely tied up with our recent survey of USP and NF preparations showing a violation of Sec. 7. I, and its regulation that a clear opinion from the Administration seems desirable."

72. A. G. Murray, Memorandum for Mr. Larrick, 4 June 1932. C. W. Crawford, Letter to Western District Chief, 4 June 1932. "The Eastern District has made a rather thorough canvass of this matter and finds that the mercuric chloride tablets on the market are generally not the USP article."

73. Cullen to Cook, 22 October 1932.

74. Cook to Cullen, 26 October 1932.

75. Cook to Cullen, 4 June 1932. "...Standards for Liquid Petrolatum... In the judgment of the Committee, any oil falling within the ranges named, might be properly call 'Liquid Petrolatum' and if the titles 'heavy' and 'light' oils were set up as specific official titles, the physician and pharmacist would also be required to specify, when, in fact, the physician would not likely know that there was a difference. I think you would appreciate the difficulty if the two titles were established as separate texts."

76. Cullen to Cook, 22 October 1932.

77. Cullen to Cook, 7 June 1932. "Some time ago we wrote you in regard to the advisability of permitting in the next edition of the Pharmacopoeia some latitude in the selection of ointment bases.... The United States Pharmacopoeia is supposed to be a standard for the United States and its possessions. In addition the Spanish translation is official in several countries. The revision committee should not lose sight of the fact that this volume should provide products which can be used in the tropics as well as Alaska."

78. Cook to Cullen, 15 June 1932. "I have before me your letter of June 7 in which you call our attention to the importance of permitting a modification of the fatty vehicles in ointments to meet varying climatic conditions.... The present Pharmacopoeia on Page 410 permits this for Unguentum and also on Page 103 for Ceratum."

79. A. G. Murray to Cook, 2 August 1932.

80. Cook to Murray, 4 August 1932.

81. Cook to Murray, 12 September 1932. "I greatly appreciate your critical study of the proposed definitions for extracts, fluidextracts, etc. now before the Sub-Committee No. 11...as I know of no one else so familiar with the results under the Law.... As you know, the Food and Drugs Act permits modifications of USP products, providing they are declared, but there is a trend both in the Federal Departments and some laws already enacted in the States, to require that preparations sold under USP title may not be modified in any way. I believe that the manufacturers are disturbed by this trend and that they would be glad to see some leniency in these general statements in the Pharmacopocia."

82. Murray to Cook, 31 August 1932.

83. Murray to Cook, 11 October 1932.

84. Murray to Cook, 16 July 1932. "The Pharmacopoeia states that 'Pilocarpine Hydrochloride melts between 195 and 198 degrees C.' Some samples recently examined in this Administration, which meet the requirements of the Pharmacopoeia in other respects, melted several degrees above the maximum temperature mentioned. Henry states that pilocarpine hydrochloride melts at 204-205 degrees C. Two of our samples melted near 203 degrees uncorrected (208 degrees corrected). Helpful information as to the melting point of this drug can doubtless be supplied by the manufacturers of it."

85.   Murray to Cook, 30 August 1932.

86.   Cook to Murray, 1 September 1932.

87.   Cook to Murray, 12 September 1932.

88.   Murray to Cook, 14 December 1932.

89.   Murray to Cook, 15 December 1932.

90.   Murray to Gathercoal, 24 May 1933, GC, 1933 decimal file 500.42. "...'When-dried-to-constant-weight' basis for the rubrics of salts.... The physician ought to know as near as practicable just what his patient is receiving in a preparation, not what he would have received if the ingredients had been dried before the prescription was filled...there is no requirement that the ingredients be dried before being weighed. This introduces an element of uncertainty in the composition of preparations for which no rubric is provided. When the rubrics for the ingredients are indefinite the finished product can not be held to a definitive requirement as to composition.... The rubric for lithium bromide as given in the National Formulary is still more indefinite since it provides for as much as 15% of water even after the salt has been dried...unless the Pharmacopoeia and the National Formulary provide suitable standards for the salts themselves, it seems to us it will be impossible to provide any reasonable tolerance for the preparations unless it is required that the ingredients themselves are assayed before the preparations are manufactured and that the formulas be based on the results of those assays, rather than upon definite weights of the salts as they are found in commerce.... Do you think it would be advisable to introduce a test for chloride in the various bromides to limit the proportions permitted?"

91.   Cook to Murray, 25 October 1932, GC, 1932 decimal file 500.41.

92.   Murray to Cook, 31 May 1932. "Is it not undesirable to define the Pharmacopoeia article [quinine and quinidine] in terms of an unstable form if the reasonable stable form can be defined." Murray to Cook, 30 August 1932. "The rubric for sodium chloride has been raised to 99.5% based upon the dried weight. Should not some limit for moisture be provided? I am under the impression quite a low limit for moisture could be specified."

93.   Murray to Cook, 15 October 1932.

94.   Cook to Murray, 2 June 1932.

95.   Cullen to Gathercoal, 10 June 1933, GC, 1933 decimal file 500.42. "N.F. Sub-Committee No. 8...'It should also be kept in mind that an aqueous extract of ergot, made up with acidified water and assaying about four times the strength of Standard Fluidextract of Ergot is now being marketed'.... We are not familiar with this preparation and would appreciate it if you will kindly give us the name of such preparations."

96.   Gathercoal to Cullen, 27 June 1933.

97.   Cullen to Gathercoal, 7 August 1933. "No where in the label statements of this preparation is mention made that the product is an aqueous extract of ergot."

98.   Gathercoal to Cullen, 10 August 1933.

99.   W. T. McClosky to F. E. Bibbins, 15 August 1933.

100. Bibbins to McClosky, 12 September 1933.

101. Cullen to Gathercoal, 23 September 1933.

102. Record Group 16 (RG16), NARA, Office of the Solicitor: Legal Opinions—1910-1937.

103. W. G. Campbell, 1932 Fraud School Report, 2 July 1932, GC, 1932 decimal file 505.1. His memorandum details the history of fraud and amendments to the 1906 Act.

104. Campbell to Gathercoal, 10 July 1936, GC, 1936 decimal file 500.42.

105. Durrett to Gathercoal, 6 August 1931, GC, 1931 decimal file 500.42. "Mr. B. A. Linden of the Bacteriological laboratory of this Administration…. Under 'Solution of Carbofuchsin' suggests that the term 'Fuchsin' be modified to 'Basic Fuchsin.'"
106. Cullen to Gathercoal, 25 May 1933, GC, 1933 decimal file 500.42. "…In harmony with other suggestions we have made relating to the use of therapeutically significant designations for official drugs, we are now suggesting that this synonym be dropped in the forthcoming revision."
107. Cullen to Gathercoal, 18 August 1933. "'Dentrifice' and 'toothache drugs'…We presume the names of these items will be suitably modified so as not to deny the use of these common designations to non-official articles…'zinc paste without salicylic acid'…reserving the designation 'zinc paste' for the new article…"
108. Cullen to Gathercoal, 29 November 1933.
109. E. F. Cook, A revision of the test for dextrose (dextrin) and sucrose under lactose in the USP X, 1932, RG88, NARA, General correspondence—1919-1937, 1932 decimal file 500.41; H. S. Paine, Memorandum to A.G. Murray, 17 June 1932.
110. George Denton Beal was the 23rd Remington Medallist. See Griffenhagen supra note 19 at 110-8.
111. Campbell to Gathercoal, 10 July 1936, GC, 1936 decimal file 500.42; Gathercoal to Campbell, 13 July 1936.
112. Durrett to Gathercoal, 18 July 1936.

Dénouement

Defining Drugs: Consequences of Seeking External Governance

I call this ending a dénouement because it posits the outcome of a very complicated series of events regarding drug therapy. Normally, in a scholarly work of history, the ending is called "epilogue." Alternatively, anthropology scholarship ends as a "conclusion." I will leave it for my readers to decide the appropriate label.

In the last chapter, "Negotiating Reality," the evolving arbiter role of the federal government through the Bureau of Chemistry and Food and Drug Administration was examined. Interaction between government (chemists, pharmacologists, and administrators) and private citizens in professional groups found in the general correspondence files of the Bureau of Chemistry and FDA illustrated the influence of government over the writing of enforceable standards for pharmaceutical therapies.

In the dénouement (epilogue or conclusion), I discuss the social consequences that pertain to: (1) the expansion of political rights for practitioners and producers; and (2) a shifted responsibility for therapeutic consequences from individual practitioners to government. In addition, in light of present estimates of systemic drug-related morbidity and mortality, implications for the future will focus on three common historical themes. First, "Reform" will examine continued efforts by the federal government to arbitrate pharmaceutical fact and rationalize pharmacotherapy for the purposes of the state. Second, "Rights and responsibilities" of citizens as producers and consumers of therapeutic agents will focus on the praxeology of human action. Last, "Definition of drug therapy—governmental vs. cultural" will explore the nature of drug use in a free society, and, with particular reference to the therapeutic applications of discoveries from the Human Genome Project, the limitations of "statute" to assure responsive treatment by practitioners.

Pharmaceutical Fact Revisited

Pharmaceutical fact is the negotiated construction of an idealized socio-legal meaning of drug therapy in terms of: (1) what should be produced; (2) who should produce; (3) who should recommend; (4) who should distribute; and (5) who should consume. It describes how the social control of drug therapy came to be thought of in society, divorced from particular individuals or material facts. Coercion is intimately linked with the twentieth-century conception of drug therapy.

At the beginning of the twentieth century, these questions were determined by an individual practitioner, by the person who either needed therapeutic remediation or used drugs, or by free exchange and mutual consent of both parties. As the process of "doctoring" differentiated into a specialized division of labor, separation between individual activities as producer and consumer led to formalized rules for participation. Groups seeking control of these formalized rules negotiated with government for their consistent enforcement. Each group needed a set of standards to adjudicate the sacred, natural, and true from the profane, artificial, and false. These separations, propelled by evolving federal enforcement and funded by a shift from tariffs to employment taxation, created a durable social system for the use of drug therapy.

There can be no standards for pharmaceuticals without an end-use, like therapy, in mind. The facts about medicinal substances are inseparably tied to their potential benefits in individual patients. Government became the "decider" of that potential, and placed a numerical onus of proof on manufacturers prior to marketing their medicinal substances.

Mises posited the idea that human social conduct, including action and cooperation, derives from an overall interpretation of life, what he called a worldview. However, what made that worldview real and actionable for individuals was an ideology. It is through an actual interpretation of all the events in an individual's life held in that context that the idea of worldview functions effectively in guiding action. A worldview, by itself, does not suffice. All individuals act in the world, not in their minds.

What Wiebe called "the search for order"—by producers and consumers, citizens and government alike—continued throughout the early twentieth century. Standards-setting activities were, at first, entrusted to professionals by government. As professional standards continued to fall short of enforcement, officials in the Department of Agriculture, especially pharmacologists and chemists, began to question the reliability and validity of the rubrics of medicine and pharmacy. The rubrics were not sufficient in the detail required for the federal government to exercise police power, to seize property, to apprehend and prosecute offenders, or to render justice. Near the end of the period, beginning in 1933, Rexford Tugwell led the executive charge to remedy the failings of the Pure Food and Drugs Act of 1906. Government, not voluntary professional associations and corporations, would become the arbiter of pharmaceutical fact regarding scope and therapeutics. This sentiment was echoed by many professional leaders who had direct experience of the social maladaptation codified in the 1906 Act.

The historical repositories of individual and social facts have provided insight into how the federal government became the arbiter of pharmaceutical fact. The evolution of this social system vested political and economic power in scientific achievement. Further, that social system allowed science-based practitioners the license within their scope of practice to set standards that the government would enforce. This system gave professionals many "rights," but essentially absolved them from responsibilities for the ongoing evaluation of pharmacotherapy in individuals. As a major consequence of professional negotiation, the federal government assumed control of standards and arbitration of pharmaceutical fact over the study's forty-year period.

About history, Carr noted:[1]

> The facts of history are indeed facts about individuals, but not about actions of individuals performed in isolation, and not about the motives, real or imaginary, from which individuals suppose themselves to have acted. They are facts about the relations of individuals to one another in society and about the social forces which produce from the actions of individuals results often at variance with, and sometimes opposite to, the results which they themselves intended.

Prior historiography by Dupree, Hofstadter, and Wiebe documented the dichotomous worldview held by many intellectuals and regulatory idealists. That worldview was then translated into action-oriented ideologies to direct the medicalization of virtue and the criminalization of vice with respect to citizens' self-selected drug use. Narcotic, alcohol, and venereal disease control efforts resulted from legislation designed by professional groups to circumscribe their jurisdictions, and from regulations promulgated by the evolving police apparatus of the federal government.

Scope and therapeutics constituted the negotiated, social struc- ture for standards. The polity, or social structure, of standards-set- ting emanated both from government and from professional organi- zations like the United States Pharmacopoeial Convention Commit- tee of Revision, AMA's Council on Pharmacy and Chemistry, and APhA's Committee on Unofficial Remedies and National Formulary Committee. Federal law was written in 1906 that vested political power in the standards of the USP and National Formulary. While James H. Beal publicly always gave credit to Harvey Wiley, pri- vately he took pride in realizing the inefficiency of government- directed codification of standards, and the achievement of official investiture of pharmacy-controlled standards.

Very active in the drive for enactment of the 1906 Act, American medical leaders were left out of the initial transfiguration of stan- dards to statute brought about by USP and NF. An ensuing thirty- year battle with organized pharmacy would begin to dominate interprofessional discussion, often leading to deeper separations over pharmacopoeial scope and rational therapeutics.

Themes of citizenship and patienthood were woven throughout the book. Requirements for citizenship in the New Nation coincided with the appearance of direct representation and the "unraveling of the clan society" into competing ideologies for social control. Those considered less than full citizens with different beliefs and uses for pharmaceutical agents were routinely marginalized and demonized regarding their drug use.

Government regulation throughout this period was largely devoted to modulating the factors and means of production, not with deriv- ing a set of consumption rules for consumers. There is compelling evidence that professional groups desired exclusive control of sci- entific expert standards, and implored government to enforce the distinctions from which they benefited. Pharmaceutical fact, as phar- macopoeial scope and rational therapeutics, contributed to the ex- pansion of the national economy by creating demand and codifying commerce. In response to rampant empiricism throughout the nine- teenth century, many professional leaders idealized about law and practice pertaining to pharmacotherapy, and created standards in the context of personally available evidence.

However genuinely concerned with human misery and economic fraud, "producers" convinced government that "consumers" needed them to continue to create standards. To government, standards for drugs and their therapeutic application came to be thought of as guarantees of integrity and propriety. Substances were legislated and codified into federal existence, and defined in terms of enforcement. What started as a simple statement about food purity evolved into a complex social system where all stakeholders (except end-users, citizen-patients) lobbied for their version of the sacred, true, and natural. All other contrary behavior and action was, by definition, criminal. The processes of alcohol and narcotic use initially generated revenue for the National government (contributing to the elimination of the tariff system). However, use of these substances that was not directed by medical and pharmacy professionals from an enforceable legal code for some therapeutic end of the practitioner's choice became illegal.

Evidence presented in the Beal-Kremers correspondence supports the contention that many leaders believed that individuals had to be patients in order to use drugs. Academic pharmacists like Beal and Kremers advocated for law that would elevate rank and file members to a scientific pharmaceutical practice. Beal crafted the practicability of the Harrison Act through the National Drug Trade Conference as well as the Pure Food and Drugs Act through the National Food and Drug Congress.

Federal law had to be consistent with the Constitution and international treaties to which the United States was a signatory. The 1906 Act provided the regulatory basis of fact for the substances covered under the Harrison Act. The Harrison Act determined the conditions under which narcotics would be used, and separated physicians and pharmacists with respect to record keeping and prescriptions. Government operatives oppressed individual citizens (both producers and consumers) by incarceration and seizure of wealth because of inappropriate and irrational drug use.

To Kremers and Beal, pharmacy deserved professional status. Education and legislation would achieve this objective, and would provide pharmacists with the benefits afforded to medicine and law. Because they were in harmony on educational and legislative issues, most of their correspondence concerned their differences. Primarily, these differences related to the type of social control to be exerted by government on the professions. As pharmaceutical standards became resolved as to the qualifications of persons for the practice of pharmacy, their disagreements (if one could call them that) were about drug therapy as an article of commerce and trade.

Kremers seemed to favor "professional" service while Beal sided with the commercial aspects of pharmaceutical production. They were in agreement about narcotic control because it was perceived to benefit the professional and commercial sides of pharmacy, and society at large. They shared the idea of the profession's advancement through elevation of educational and legislative standards they presumed would continue under direct professional control. When the federal government began to assume control of standards by providing reference assays in the 1920s, Kremers continued arguments for professionalization and educational reform through the bachelor's degree. Conversely, Beal increased his activities with commercial organizations like the United States Chamber of Commerce and NARD while maintaining leadership of the Board of Trustees of the United States Pharmacopoeial Convention.

Control of narcotic use through the Harrison Act was the first application of federal police power to directly affect the practices of pharmacy and medicine. The Pure Food and Drugs Act had provided the statutory basis for the standards of narcotics as determined by the USP. To federal officials, the USP was perceived as a quasi-legislative functionary with the full force of law. State laws were then harmonized with both federal statutes, coinciding with uniform requirements for education and reciprocity of licensure for pharmacists. James Beal presided over the "legislative" negotiating structure for standards as chairman of the USP Board of Trustees and as pharmaceutical statesman. Edward Kremers supplied the scientific arguments that guided many of Beal's legal positions.

Tensions between physicians and pharmacists, as seen through the lens of the American Social Hygiene Association, provided insight into the interplay of virtue and vice. Narcotic and alcohol control were two components of social hygiene: Another major issue was control of venereal disease. The primary tension was generated from what came to be seen as unethical practices in both professional groups: dispensing doctors and counter-prescribing pharmacists.

During the 1920s, private philanthropy and public health-minded physicians saw great advantages to a legally mandated system of drug therapy. Academic pharmacy was in favor of law that would place physicians' prescriptions in the hands of pharmacists and thereby reduce or eliminate pharmacists' financial dependence on the sale of non-drug merchandise. Because many physicians either did not write out their prescriptions or sold patent medicines, pharmacists often treated patients with venereal disease without referral to physicians in the established practice called "counter-prescribing." Advocating for a physician-directed drug therapy system, ASHA sought to improve relations between public health and private practice by making drug therapy the sole legal prerogative of physicians even though many could not administer treatments properly.

Dispensing doctors and counter-prescribing pharmacists were opposite sides of the same empirical coin. Evidence from the records of the American Social Hygiene Association illustrated the problems of treating venereal disease through an undifferentiated, unauthorized drug therapy system.

The "quackery" situation was similar in all parts of the country whether there were many exacting laws that governed the practice (New Orleans and Kansas City) or a few vague ones (Chicago, New York City, and Newark). Upholding AMA's idea of "quackery," ASHA sought to provide both evidence and polemic that would behoove local, state, and national authorities to enact stronger laws and enforce existing laws that sanctioned the initiation of pharmacotherapy only under certain circumstances. That context for therapy had several characteristics by default: (1) face-to-face dialogue between patient and allopathic physician; (2) no advertising or solicitation; (3) no mention or guarantees of cure; and (4) separate prescribing and dispensing activities specified by law.

No level of government could ensure "pure" drugs recommended and administered as a therapeutic intervention by professionals who knew what they were doing. The federal government was able to enforce the medical context in which citizens received narcotics, and thereby control that aspect of the nostrum trade. Use of narcotics under any other circumstances was illegal. Despite the efforts of Surgeon General Thomas Parran, venereal disease control was medically possible, and cure approachable, only by requiring the safety of pharmaceuticals in the aftermath of the sulfanilamide tragedy.

The mechanisms of control of the therapeutic process outside of the process itself became firmly institutionalized with narcotics, alcohol, and venereal diseases because of their connection with vice. The medical police concept had motivated many public health campaigns. However, by injecting police power into an evolving structure of medical authority over therapeutics, a false sense of propriety and security about drug therapy approved by government only magnified the weaknesses of individual responsibility, a fear that dominated Progressive-like reforms. Thus, venereal disease laws were not effective in addressing socially acceptable forms of treatment despite considerable advances in scientific therapies like neoarsphenamine. However, it is interesting to note that sulfonamides became the object of government efforts to enforce pre-market safety of drug products at the same time the sulfonamides offered a pharmaceutical cure for syphilis.

The federal government's commercial policies in the 1920s allowed businessmen and professionals to set their own standards of operation. The Market Crash brought this policy into serious question. Government held standards-setting groups accountable for the standards they had created. Regulators continually appealed to professional and business leaders within medicine and pharmacy for numerically based rubrics. Manufacturers supported a legally mandated system of drug therapy because it increased sales and reduced the expense of direct consumer advertising.

Correspondence between federal officials in the Food and Drug Administration and leaders in the USP and NF revision committees was presented to illustrate the tensions between pharmaceutical producers. The resolution of this tension, which culminated in the Copeland Bill (the federal Food, Drug, and Cosmetic Act of 1938), established the federal government as arbiter of both pharmacopoeial scope and rational therapeutics.

The federal government could not uniformly enforce the descriptive rubrics of professional bodies despite an elaborate system of local-state-federal cooperation Harvey W. Wiley and his successors expanded. Pharmaceutical manufacturers and compounding practitioners alike exploited the vagaries of federal law by inventing and producing substances for therapeutic application whose regulation was not covered under existing statutes. Government scientists continually negotiated with organization leaders to create quantitative standards based on the results of evolving experimental science. Unless official standards could be applied universally for the purposes of governing trade, their specifications left regulators in search of other mechanisms, like the Federal Specifications Board and engineering groups, to reconcile the differences between standard and statute.

Harvey Wiley's tempestuous leadership set the tone of enforcement and tutored many regulators who followed him, those who believed in the merits of a cooperative relationship between government and the professions. The constitutional basis for the enforcement of standards would be questioned repeatedly in the decade following enactment of the pre-marketing safety provisions of the Copeland Bill. Vacillating between science and law, both government officials and professional leaders negotiated the evolving numerical facts. They translated those facts about scope and therapeutics into a social system that rationalized the application of physical force. The unit of measure became the label.

Government regulators increasingly pressured pharmacists E. Fullerton Cook of the United States Pharmacopoeia and Edmund N. Gathercoal of the National Formulary to revise many aspects of official compendia. Bureau officials were impatient with the lack of progress in changing the rubrics, especially after the USP assumed from FDA the distribution and production of reference bioassays. Industrial production of new synthetic compounds clearly changed the focus of government interaction with the revision committees, and magnified deficiencies of scientific currency and accuracy as well as successful enforcement of compendial standards.

Allowable variation with respect to official names, stated tolerances for assay and potency, physical properties, therapeutic dosages, and descriptions for measurement were recommended by chemists, pharmacologists, and bacteriologists when it made their regulation and/or industrial production more efficient. Strict conditions for the use of official names resulted from widespread misuse and the movement among several states to create independent statutes. Mushrooming into big business, the specific conditions for drug trading and therapy would become codified through later amendments to the federal Food, Drug, and Cosmetic Act of 1938. Those amendments detailed who would have statutory authority to manufacture, initiate, distribute, and modify a newly encoded federal entity: prescription drug therapy.

The Consequences

The major consequences of seeking external governance of drug therapy are experienced daily in American society. The political rights established for practitioners and producers came at the expense of other citizens. The responsibility for the therapeutic consequences of drug therapy shifted from individual practitioners to government. As a result, a rationalized process of care developed that divorced standards of scope and therapeutics from their identification in individual patients.

Government was interested initially in certifying the means, not the purpose or goals, of treatment for citizens. The federal government focused its regulatory efforts on the substances used in medicinal therapies. State governments regulated the practitioners of pharmacy and medicine (at their behest) through licensure requirements.

Since the application of Post Office fraud statutes to medical claims after the Civil War, the federal government has always held an intense regulatory interest in who could claim to cure diseases with pharmacotherapy.[2] Curing disease and curbing vice have had great political value for the state in the twentieth century, leading to various "wars," such as the National Cancer Institute's assault on cancer and the latest war on "drugs." The 1912 Sherley amendment testifies to the political power vested in bringing about a very desirable "outcome"—a cure.

Let us now consider the implications when government or industry designs treatment purposes and "outcomes" for individuals. In the introduction, it was argued that cooperative research and treatment by science and government was undertaken in the national interest. Government did not need to own the means of production if it could control the direction and application. Government financing of research and treatment became a major method for this control. Third-party financing mechanisms will likely continue to drive a shift from medical necessity in individuals to political entitlement in groups. As a methodology for identifying sources of cost without benefit, Clancy and Eisenberg discussed individual outcomes from health care as the necessary, but missing, component for effective third-party decision making. Measuring outcomes is a multidimensional, metric-intensive process that is purported to "shape opportunities for patients to be co-managers of their health and health care."[3] Access to therapies may be achieved as a result of one's identification as a member of an industry-defined, government-sanctioned disease-related group. Competition for resources between disease-related groups may become a key political issue at the federal level.

Each group will likely advocate for a combined budget of research and treatment, and will collect outcomes information in terms of cost and benefit in order to justify expenditures. Recent examples of disease-related political entitlements include end-stage renal disease, cancer, diabetes, and acquired immune deficiency syndrome.

Other groups will likely organize for their share of resource allocation, especially when genetic information is pooled for political purposes. Government will accept responsibility for a group's genetic make-up, and will insist on treatments that it has certified and validated as cost-effective.

The major consequence of seeking outside governance is that government approval of drug therapy has diluted the responsibilities of both practitioners and citizens to engage in therapeutic vigilance. In the industrial model of drug therapy, Fuchs discussed the lack of post-marketing surveillance and a truncated pharmacist-physician relationship as major reasons for problems with drug therapy.[4] Official pronouncements of purpose, safety, and effectiveness may be upheld in randomized clinical trials involving discrete populations, but not in individual treatment. Citizens have drug therapy problems, in part, because no one is monitoring recommendations and actions in the context of individual biological variation. Objective standards of proof and value are the individual patient's response to drug therapy resulting from individual choice and application.

Government approval of the use of pharmaceutical therapy does not currently extend to the individual treatment level. However, customization of pharmaceutical design using the results of genome research could have significant effects on individuals and their families.[5] Practitioners and patients have therapeutic latitude in determining whether drugs will be used within the scope of official labeling. But, as marginal cost is identified, quantified, and associated with marginal use, it is likely that choice will be restricted to authorized purposes.

Reforming Therapeutic Reform?

The compelling reason for investigating how government became the arbiter of pharmaceutical fact is because of the pandemic nature of drug-related morbidity and mortality in the late twentieth century. Why drug therapy became a problem of such magnitude is not as clear today as the death of E. Fullerton Cook's friend of accidental mercury poisoning in 1932. He selected the wrong bottle of tablets in a darkened room.

I have argued that the socio-legal system of drug therapy may have institutionalized morbidity and mortality, and implied that practitioners in this system are not held accountable and responsible for their actions involving the drug therapy of individuals. Indeed, given the evidence, government approval of "magic bullets' recommended by "informed intermediaries" engenders a tenuous sense of security about purpose, safety, and effectiveness when disconnected from events in particular patients' lives.

Pharmaceutical fact embodies a normative component about how drugs get from discovery to therapy. How shall drugs be used? It describes a rationalized construct divorced from the material existence of any substance's properties. The professions and industry have had their opportunities to guide the social ideation of drug therapy argued here as pharmaceutical fact. Drug-related morbidity and mortality are in-built defects that are institutionalized in the social system of drug therapy.

What constitutes proof and value depends on who asks the question. It was thought that the union of the professions and government would provide assured answers to questions of proof and value to citizens. Professionals convinced government officials that citizens were largely too ignorant to make decisions for self-medication.

Even after passage of the Copeland Bill, federal government officials continued to assert that federal law was designed to promote self-treatment. But, as rank and file practitioners in medicine and pharmacy continued to recommend nostrums, and citizens continued to use them, academic physicians and pharmacists argued for increased federal involvement in two different, but complementary, ways. Academic physicians lobbied for increased federal funding for their university-based scientific research. Academic pharmacists worked for state and federal legislation to professionalize their commercial practices, and to keep them separate from the practice of medicine. This heightened intervention, indirect by physicians and direct by pharmacists, institutionalized the "informed intermediary" process.

The first therapeutic reformation set the stage for commercial exploitation of nature through scientific problem solving enforced by the federal government. The descriptive rubrics of standards-setting organizations embodied a conceptual understanding of drug therapy founded on sense perception. These perceptual-conceptual rubrics came under increasingly negative comment from regulators, scientists, and industry. Instead of these organoleptic concepts, operationalized constructions of pharmaceutical fact were enforceable by law because they could be numerically measured by experimental science.

Direct sense perception introduced individual bias and produced vague definitions of existential properties. In contrast, idealized, rationalized definitions and standards were formed from the results of detached, disinterested experimentation with a hypothetical population for a delimited purpose. But, as Marks pointed out, everyone involved was interested in the results of science.[6] To some, sensory perception was the epistemological equivalent of vice. Learned, moral men determined standards of scientific practice, and could rationalize their conflicts of interest. Nature revealed by science was too complicated to be understood by average citizens.

These same arguments about individual practitioner or citizen ignorance and inability to choose appropriate courses of action are forwarded today to justify increased governmental involvement in genetic research. Experts hold that therapeutic intervention must have even more oversight to minimize exploitation of citizens by commercial producers and practitioners. Knoppers, Hirtle, and Glass discussed four different policy-making approaches to address commerce in human genetic material: (1) human rights; (2) statutory; (3) administrative; and (4) market-driven. The first three approaches entail governmental solutions through judicial, legislative, and executive functions upheld by police power.[7] Idealists have often rationalized an ethic of government controls that have had the political effect of expropriating rights by preventing self-interested choices. As Illich noted in 1976: [8]

> Most of the remedies now proposed by social engineers and economists to reduce iatrogenesis include a further increase of medical controls...they render clinical, social, and cultural iatrogenesis self-reinforcing.

If idealism in standards setting and control continues unabated, the next therapeutic reformation might well make possible the sanctioned commercial exploitation of patients. The federal government allowed the pharmaceutical industry to become a thriving, protected cartel, provided it served the general welfare interests of the state. State governments allowed professions to define the boundaries of their monopolies by statute, provided they met the requirements of public health.

As science funded by the federal government continues to identify and quantify genetic sequences discovered in the Human Genome Project,[9] ideas of virtue and vice that led to the first drug therapy controls for narcotics, alcohol, and venereal disease could be applied to individuals who resist their own genetic identification and manipulation. Perhaps government's position in the next century may be that moral citizens should desire and deserve health at any cost of life, liberty, or money.

Is it even possible to reform therapeutic reform? There are many more disincentives to reform today because of the nature of precedents and the constituencies that developed around them. But, the idea of reforming reform is itself an idealized notion. The only true reform of a reform is repeal. Instead of striking a balance among competing group interests, perhaps the federal government should uphold the policy that the right of every individual to freely associate shall not be abrogated.

Rights and Responsibilities

The institutional process of regulating pharmaceutical therapy in America began with learned arguments involving purity. In an era of vice control, narcotic use and venereal disease treatment further galvanized the cultural meaning of drug use in legal terms. Appeals for government control were couched in ways that government was evolving at the federal level to resolve social problems: Authenticate what could be enforced; seize, prosecute, and criminalize what could not be authenticated.

From Progressivism to the New Deal, a false dichotomy developed: the political separation of those that produced and those that consumed. Producers and consumers alike began to believe that their rights superseded their rights as citizens. Producers believed their right to produce included: (1) what products and services would be invented; (2) what standard would be employed; (3) what products and services would be called; (4) to whom would they sell products and services; (5) what price would be asked; (6) who would resell their products; (7) and under what conditions would products and services be used. Consumers believed that their right to consume included what grades of products and services would be available, what would be purchased, what price would be paid, and how products would be used.

Pharmacists wanted the right to an independent profession separate from medicine. They wanted to set the standards for drugs, and to maintain and strengthen their "keeper of the drugs" role. Physicians wanted sole authority for the use of drugs as therapeutic intervention within the context of a private healing relationship with patients.

In seeking a resolution to these social tensions, professional groups negotiated first among themselves. As industrial mass manufacturing created new therapeutic agents, property rights entered into the social calculus. Drug therapy had become a commodity, an article of trade. Manufacturers often asserted their right to sell products to agents of their choice by labeling them as prescription. Industry then lobbied the federal government to make the prescription drug a compulsory entitlement under its own control.

However, the right to produce does not entail a corresponding responsibility to consume. Conversely, the right to consume does not mean the responsibility to produce. The very notion of separate political rights to produce and to consume could indicate that constitutional rights were afforded to individuals, not as a state of their being, but in relation to their performance of state-sanctioned actions in segmented groups. Nevertheless, although a derivative of production, consumption was considered of lesser importance.

But, standards of pharmacopoeial scope and rational therapeutics could not be separated from the above praxeological considerations involving acting people. Action was an integrated process of production and consumption for those who set standards as well as for everyone else. Standards served the professions whose practices were believed to require government protection from the uneducated. After every act and amendment at the federal level, prices for drug therapy increased because the availability of options decreased. Many professional groups began to see themselves, not their patients, as ultimate consumers because they recommended or dispensed the production of industry.

Biotechnology and genetic products have the potential to cure disease and forever alter the tissue construction in an individual's body. Evans and Relling discussed the how the use of pharmacogenomics could provide a more rational scientific approach for optimizing drug therapy by identifying individual differences in enzymes, transporters, and receptors.[10] Biotechnology may bring about a reversal of the idea of virtue and vice related to drug use. The use of narcotics and other nostrums by whatever means was considered vice. In this century, drug use sanctioned to cure diseases by the federal government may become virtuous: Non-use may become vice.

Drug-related morbidity and mortality are embedded in the social system of regulating pharmaceutical therapy. It would seem prudent to direct systematic change toward what each individual patient achieves as a result of using pharmaceutical therapy and away from "absolute" therapeutic standards enforced by government. However, if historical and legal precedents are any indication of future direction, the system is set for government to impose therapeutic outcomes of industrial and professional design on its citizens. As happened with prior federal legislation, both professionals and industry may seek government enforcement of the endpoints that citizens achieve with drug therapy.

Patienthood will again be certified, but not through the revenue generating methodology of narcotic use or the gentleman's agreement between pharmacists and physicians for venereal diseases. Patients could be certified through informed consent and contractual obligations that require their training and adherence to population-based cost-effective regimens. Deviation from these therapies may be considered too morally and financially expensive for society. Nevertheless, the social system of regulating pharmaceutical therapy currently serves the interests of everyone, except individual patients. Governing in a free society is designed to safeguard citizens and their property from invasion and expropriation. Any other function it performs generally favors one segment of citizens over another. In the context of pharmaceutical fact, producers and practitioners were favored over consumers and patients.

As an approach to addressing drug-related morbidity and mortality, pharmaceutical care holds great potential.[11] It makes pharmaceutical therapy both personalized and goal-directed for individual patients, and requires practitioner accountability to each patient for problem resolution.

However, pharmacy organizations have a heritage of seeking legal remedy to afford membership protection from commercial encroachment by grocers, hardware dealers, and dispensing doctors. Pharmaceutical care can be practiced by anyone willing and able to be responsible for drug therapy problems. The commercial viability of pharmaceutical care will, no doubt, attract other non-pharmacists. As with the physical objects of pharmaceutical therapy, many pharmacy organizations may seek to protect the profession's perceived right to practice pharmaceutical care from the intellectual competition of other professional groups.

Definition of Drug Therapy—Governmental vs. Cultural?

Periodically, government has established control mechanisms to direct the course of drug therapies throughout society. The history of biologics control clearly illustrates government attempts to monopolize vaccine production. Narcotic maintenance clinics established a mechanism for dealing with substance dependence when private practices were deemed illegal. Treatment of venereal diseases through public health departments offered citizens access to government-qualified practitioners who were capable of administering intravenous injections of arsenicals. Interstate commerce has and will be used by individuals in state and federal governments to justify virtually any restriction of individually chosen economic exchanges. The Food and Drug Administration is currently testing its statutory authority in proposing the regulation of the Internet in relation to self-selected therapeutic choices.

Precedents such as these are powerful devices in the argument for more federal government control of drug therapies. However, historically, governments and industry have engaged in many experiments at the expense of captive populations for some presumed benefit of the broader society, military and public health experiments notwithstanding. [12] Genetic therapies will challenge the idea of privacy in life and property. Fuller and colleagues noted:[13] "A particular person's genetic information may be of interest to a wide variety of individuals and organizations." "Routine" care may evolve into a series of "controlled" experiments for the primary benefit of society.

Martin I. Wilbert outlined the government's position on self-medication.[14] Morbidity and mortality from the use of potent drugs was known to occur from acute or chronic poisoning. Drug laws were recognized as "economic measures designed to prevent dishonest practices or gross adulteration."[15] "Public health would be enhanced by ensuring a reputable source of supply" from "licensed druggists."[16] Moreover, he argued that "...the inherent right to self-medicate is limited by the broader and more comprehensive rights of the community at large..." especially regarding infectious and contagious diseases.

> Proper legal procedure may be invoked to prevent an individual doing himself permanent injury if the interests of the community are in any way involved.[17]

The incidence and prevalence of drug-related morbidity and mortality provide a graphic illustration that the federal government cannot ensure the proper use, safety, or effectiveness of drug therapy for individuals. Moreover, a government-sanctioned system of professional treatment has failed to protect citizens from the unintended consequences of drug therapy.

Why was self-medication, a cultural definition and determination of drug therapy, perceived as inadequate? Free choice and reciprocity were inimical to state planning and problem-solving.[18] Individual choice is not predictable, and often not in the interests of the state. The federal government will likely expect the application of results from the investment in the Human Genome Project to yield predictable outcomes—cures.

A formal partnership between practitioners of pharmacy and medicine committed to responsive pharmacotherapy was one option suggested at the turn of the last century to retain standards within a therapeutic context. Instead, organized pharmacy opted for the path of legal codification of commerce that would include pharmacists in the political economy of drug distribution.

It is not clear why pharmacists in the USP resisted the inclusion of therapeutic choice in the official compendia. Perhaps the separation of the functions of pharmacy and medicine perpetuated morbidity and mortality from pharmaceutical therapy. Perhaps retailing in drugs as a commodity developed because physicians and pharmacists did not practice therapeutics together. Perhaps citizens placed inordinate faith in scientific medicine.

Free association would provide citizens with the opportunity to deal with anyone of their choice regarding their health. It would be up to each individual to decide the course of action most suited to one's life and goals. No one would be restricted by third party obligations in procuring their pharmaceutical therapies from any source.

Government became the arbiter of pharmaceutical fact because the professions of pharmacy and medicine, as well as the pharmaceutical industry, could enforce their standards only through police powers reserved to government. With the power of physical force, by a series of segmentations, government would ensure science-based value trading in a social system for regulating pharmaceuticals and their therapeutic application. "Producer" citizens achieved their political rights at the expense of others' rights of association, speech, and property.

Notes

1.   Carr, 1961: 64.
2.   Kebler, 1922: 678-683.

3.   Clancy and Eisenberg, 1998: 245-246. As a methodology for identifying sources of cost without benefit, the authors discussed individual outcomes from health care as the necessary, but missing, component for effective third-party decision-making. Measuring outcomes is a multi-dimensional, metric intensive process that is purported to "shape opportunities for patients to be co-managers of their health and health care."

4.   In the industrial model of drug therapy, Fuchs (1974: 105-126) discussed the lack of post-marketing surveillance and a truncated pharmacist-physician relationship as major reasons for problems with drug therapy.

5.   Greely, 1998: 473-502.

6.   Marks, 1997: 229-238.

7.   Knoppers, Hirtle, Glass (1999: 2277-2278) discussed four different policy-making approaches to address commerce in human genetic material: (1) human rights; (2) statutory; (3) administrative; and (4) market-driven. The first three approaches entail governmental solutions through judicial, legislative, and executive functions upheld by police power.

8.   Illich, 1976.

9.   Collins, Patrinos, Jordan et al., 1998: 682-689.

10.   Evans and Relling (1999: 487-491) discussed how the use of pharmacogenomics could provide a more rational scientific approach for optimizing drug therapy by identifying individual differences in enzymes, transporters, and receptors.

11.   Cipolle, Strand, and Morley, 1998.

12.   Moreno, 1999; also Bammer, Dobler-Mikola, Flemming et al., 1999: 1277-1278, and Fairchild and Bayer, 1999: 919-921.

13.   Fuller, Ellis, Barr et al., (1999: 1359-1361) noted, "A particular person's genetic information may be of interest to a wide variety of individuals and organizations."

14.   Burkholder, 1968: 330-343.

15.   Wilbert, 1915.

16.   Wilbert, 1914.

17.   Wilbert, 1913.

18.   Mises, 1949; Balandier, 1970.

Methodology and Bibliographic Sources

The primary purpose of historical research is to provide an integrated meaning and to critically derive a context for understanding the relationship between the surviving documentation of facts and historical events and a series of events.[1] Dibble's methodology provides a set of rules for making inferences from testimony from individuals, the social bookkeeping of groups, documents as correlates of events, and documents as direct indicators of events. This methodology is based on the psychological laws governing cognition, memory, and communication.

Data sources have included primary archival sources, secondary sources reviewing primary archives, biographical archival and secondary sources, and association archives.

For primary archival sources, the National Archives II (NA II) was visited for correspondence between federal officials and professional and business organizations of the time period related to drug therapy standards. The correspondence decimal files of the Bureau of Chemistry and Food and Drug Administration are located in the National Archives at College Park, Maryland. Correspondence between 1925 and 1929 could not be located. The archives of the National Association of Boards of Pharmacy and personal papers of Edward Kremers, Robert P. Fischelis, and Francis E. Stewart housed in the Wisconsin Historical Society were examined.

The primary source for information about and the actual correspondence between James Hartley Beal and Edward Kremers is housed in the F. B. Power Memorial Library at the University of Wisconsin—Madison. The collection is commonly referred to as the "Kremers Reference Files" (KRF). KRF is a repository of historical documents, photographs, tear sheets, correspondence, drug catalogs, and other memorabilia collected first by Edward Kremers, and continued by George Urdang, Glenn A. Sonnedecker, John Parascandola, and Gregory J. Higby under the auspices of the American Institute of the History of Pharmacy (AIHP).

Kremers kept correspondence, newspaper clippings, tear sheets, photographs, and professional and personal correspondence from various individuals in alphabetical order by last name in the section labeled A2. This information was collected in order for Kremers to write two major works: (1) *The History of Pharmacy*,[2] and (2) his autobiography. The autobiography was not completed. Kremers and Urdang completed the first edition of *The History of Pharmacy* prior to Kremers' death in 1941.

The file containing Kremer's correspondence from and to James Hartley Beal is one of the largest files of the collection. Their correspondence covered the period between 1895 and 1939, and reflected the admiration, camaraderie, and vision for standards in education and legislation between two of pharmacy's great intellectual leaders of the early twentieth century.

The AIHP collection also contains the David E. Cowen Reference Files (CRF), a repository of over 6,000, hard-to-find, entries collected by an eminent pharmacy historian from the Department of History at Rutgers, the State University of New Jersey. Several early references to Beal and Kremers were found in CRF. The primary usefulness of CRF to the novice historical researcher lies in providing actual copies of difficult-to-locate manuscripts and tear sheets.

The American Social Hygiene Association papers at the University of Minnesota, Minneapolis, were examined in reference to the tensions between pharmacists and physicians, and influences of philanthropic foundations on drug therapy control of venereal disease.

Secondary source review of primary archival sources was conducted on international narcotic control from the Opium Wars (1840-1842, 1857-1860) to the Harrison Act (1914), The United States Pharmacopoeial Convention (1820-1995), the Progress of Pharmacy from the *Journal of the American Pharmaceutical Association* (1900-1940), and the American Medical Association, Council on Pharmacy and Chemistry's *Propaganda for Reform*.

Justification and Rationale for Sources and Methodology

Early twentieth-century American history was selected as the primary context, and particularly the period between the 1906 Pure Food and Drugs Act (PL 59-384) and the 1938 Food, Drug, and Cosmetic Act (PL 75-540), because issues of purity and safety, as well as collateral enforcement problems of drug therapy received sustained scientific, public, and institutional negotiation. While purity easily followed from identity of proximate principles, concern with safety was an entirely different matter. It ushered in control of therapeutics by federal police power.

The period separating the first two federal acts pertaining to drug therapy also signified a transition within the federal government from a constitutional to an institutional republic.[3] It embodied nascent collective bargaining and cultural unrest. It gave us the Eighteenth Amendment (and its repeal), designed to prohibit sale of, then control, a ubiquitous social drug, ethanol. The first lasting federal regulation regarding drug therapy occurred during the period. (Until the Biologics Control Act of 1902 [PL 57-244[, there was no systemic domestic federal control of any aspect of therapy.) Further, the ascension of cause-and-effect science and its application to promote the biomedical model profoundly shifted the meaning, exploration, and treatment of disease as something that could be "conquered." Negotiation of pharmaceutical fact first started in courts after the passage of the 1906 Act. Juries and judges were presented arguments from the government's Bureau of Chemistry because the Department of Agriculture was not empowered with rule-making authority in its 1862 organic act.

The people selected for study were leaders in pharmacy who initiated and/or transmitted major social changes regarding pharmaceutical fact.

History and anthropology are employed as disciplinary foci because drug use is a pan-cultural phenomenon with a long history of social currency. All cultures—"primitive" and "advanced" alike—honor the soteriological value of their medicaments.[4] In addition, drug therapy expresses sacred cultural values that may appear mundane to the casual observer. A polity perspective is necessary to understand any evolving social structure—whether in tandem, parallel, or series or spontaneous, planned, or mixed—and to interpret the relational tensions extant in culture which propel its achievement. The iatrogenesis of drug-related morbidity and mortality, and present federal efforts to regulate pharmaceutical therapy control, are incomprehensible without a thorough understanding of the past.

Bibliography

Abate, T. (1999). Quote from D. Lawrence, CEO of Kaiser Permanente, *San Francisco Chronicle*, 30 June.

Abbott, A. D. (1988). *The System of Professions: An Essay on the Division of Labor*. Chicago: University of Chicago Press.

Abrams, W. B. (1976). "Therapeutics and Government: 1776 and 1976." *Clinical Pharmacology and Therapeutics 20* (1): 1-5.

AMA Council on Pharmacy and Chemistry. (1916). *The Propaganda for Reform in Proprietary Medicines*, 9th edition. Chicago: American Medical Association.

Anderson, L., and Higby, G. J. (1995). *The Spirit of Voluntarism: A Legacy of Commitment and Contribution, The United States Pharmacopoeia, 1820-1995*. Rockville, MD: The United States Pharmacopoeia Convention, Inc.

Anderson Jr., O. E. (1958). *The Health of a Nation: Harvey W. Wiley and the Fight for Pure Food*. Chicago: University of Chicago Press.

Anderson, O. E. (1964). "Pioneer Statute: The Pure Food and Drugs Act of 1906." *Journal of Public Law 13* (1): 189-204.

Anon. (1852). "Report of a Joint Committee of the Philadelphia County Medical Society and the Philadelphia College of Pharmacy, Relative to Physicians' Prescriptions." *New York Journal of Pharmacy 1*: 52-8.

_____. (1903). "The Root-Ann Gang Coaching Their Pupils—The Professor Explaining the Details." *The Bowerston Weekly Patriot*, 21 May, KRF: A2, Beal, James H.

_____. (1908). "Professor Beal goes to Pittsburgh." *Bulletin of Pharmacy 22*: 317.

_____. (1909). "Minutes of the Section on Education and Legislation." *Proceedings of the American Pharmaceutical Association 57*: 629-660.

_____. (1910). "Minutes of the Section on Education and Legislation." *Proceedings of the American Pharmaceutical Association 58*: 605-610, 673-679.

_____. (1912). "J. H. Beal Recommended to Succeed Wiley." *Pharmaceutical Era* April, 1912: 275.

_____. (1914). "Professor Beal Withdraws as Editor." *Bulletin of Pharmacy 28*.

_____. (1915). "The Law and Regulations Relating to the Production, Importation, Manufacture, Compounding, Sale, Dispensing or Giving Away of Opium or Coca Leaves, Their Salts, Derivatives or Preparations." *Pharmaceutical Era 48* (3): 101-7.

_____. (1915). "Official Rulings on the Narcotic Law." *Pharmaceutical Era 48* (4): 151-3.

_____. (1915). "Preparations Exempted and Affected by Harrison Law." *Pharmaceutical Era 48* (3): 108-13.

_____. (1915). "Edison Elated over Success in Making Synthetic Phenol." *Pharmaceutical Era 48* (9): 402.

_____. (1915). "Thomas A. Edison on Dye Situation." *Pharmaceutical Era 48* (5): 199-200.

_____. (1915). "APhA Reports on 'Proprietaries.'" *Pharmaceutical Era 48* (10): 421-3.

_____. (1917). "US Bureau of Chemistry Asks Power to Fix Standards." *Pharmaceutical Era 50* (1): 11.

_____. (1919). "New Federal Narcotic Regulations." *Pharmaceutical Era 52* (5): 115-6.

_____. (1919). "How Adulterations and Misbranding Have Been Suppressed under Wartime Conditions—Research in Optical-crystallographic Methods." *Pharmaceutical Era 52* (1):   9.

_____. (1920). "Philadelphia." *Pharmaceutical Era 53* (11): 342.

_____. (1921). "Outgoing and Incoming Chiefs of the U.S. Bureau of Chemistry." *Pharmaceutical Era 54* (9): 333.

_____. (1921). "Fischelis Elected Dean of N.J.C.P." *Pharmaceutical Era 54* (8): 299.

_____. (1922). "Pharmacy and the New Chemistry." *Pharmaceutical Era 55* (2): 41-3.

_____. (1923). "Professional and Commercial Pharmacists." *Pharmaceutical Era 56* (9): 291.

_____. (1923). "Alcohol Committee Organized." *Pharmaceutical Era 56* (6): 730.

_____. (1925). "Price Cutting Deplored: Code of Ethics Urged." *Pharmaceutical Era 59* (7): 31-2.

_____. (1925). "Country Experiencing Normal Business, with Higher Prices Prevailing." *Pharmaceutical Era 61* (2): 29-30.

_____. (1925). "New Price Standardization Bill Being Framed." *Pharmaceutical Era 61*(4): 85-6.

_____. (1927). "Drug Trade Conditions: The Cause." *Pharmaceutical Era 64* (2): 21-35.

_____. (1927). "Dr. Henry Hurd Rusby: Explorer, Botanist, Educator, Author." *Pharmaceutical Era 64* (12): 341-2.

_____. (1927). "Campbell Now Director of New Administrative Unit." *Pharmaceutical Era 64* (7): 200.

_____. (1927). "Drug Trade Conditions: The Effect." *Pharmaceutical Era 64* (3): 61-4.

_____. (1929). "Turkish Opium, Culture, Production, and Export. *Pharmaceutical Era 66* (12): 56.

_____. (1929). "Multiple Seizure Principles Explained." *Pharmaceutical Era 66* (12): 357-8.

_____. (1930). "Ernest Fullerton Cook." *Pharmaceutical Era 67* (4): 97-8.

_____. (1930). "Trends in Drug Distribution." *Pharmaceutical Era 67* (9): 267-8.

_____. (1930). "Dr. Kremers Awarded Remington Honor Medal." *Pharmaceutical Era 67* (5): 139-40.

_____. (1930). "Dean Rusby Makes Last Report." *Pharmaceutical Era 67* (9): 259-60.

_____. (1934). "Substitute for Tugwell Food Bill Hailed as a Constructive Measure." *Practical Druggist*, January: 28.

_____. (1945). "James Hartley Beal, 1861-1945." *Journal of the American Pharmaceutical Association, PPE 6* (11): 344-7.

Arny, H. V. (1920). "Report on the Progress of Pharmacy." *Proceedings of the American Pharmaceutical Association 69*: 1-19.

Article XVII. (1912). Bill of Rights, ratified 16 May.

Article XIX. (1920). Bill of Rights, ratified 26 August.

Bailey, T. A. (1930). "Congressional Opposition to Pure Food Legislation, 1879-1906." *American Journal of Sociology 36*: 52-64.

Bakalar, J. B. (1984). The Historical Direction of Drug Policy. In *Drug Control in a Free Society*, J. B. Bakalar and L. Grinspoon (eds.). Cambridge: Cambridge University Press.

Bakalar, J. B., and Grinspoon, L. (1983). "Why Drug Policy is So Harsh." *Hastings Center Report 13* (4): 34-9.

_____. (1984). "Drug Control: Three Analogies." *Journal of Psychoactive Drugs 16* (2): 107-18.

Balandier, G. (1970). *Political Anthropology*. London: Allen Lane, The Penguin Press.

Bammer, G., Dobler-Mikola, A., Flemming, P. M. et al. (1999). "The Heroin Prescribing Debate: Integrating Science and Politics." *Science 284*: 1277-8.

Barkan, I. D. (1985). "Industry Invites Regulation: The Passage of the Pure Food and Drug Act of 1906." *American Journal of Public Health 75* (1): 18-26.

Bartrip, P. (1992). "A 'Pennurth of Arsenic for Rat Poison': The Arsenic Act of 1851 and the Prevention of Secret Poisoning." *Medical History 36* (53): 53-69.

Beal, G. D. (1949). "Cooperative Development of Scientific Standards." *Journal of the American Pharmaceutical Association, Scientific Edition 38* (12): 642-5.

_____. (1951). "The Basic Philosophy of Standards." *Analytical Chemistry 23*:1528-31.

Beal, J. H. (1900a). "A General Form of Pharmacy Law Suitable for Enactment by the Several States of the United States." *Proceedings of the American Pharmaceutical Association 49*: 309-19.

_____. (1900b). "The Evolution of Pharmacy Laws in the United States." *American Druggist and Pharmaceutical Record 36*: 179-80.

_____. (1901a). "A Lesson in Practical Politics." *Bulletin of Pharmacy 15* (1): 64-7.

_____. (1901b). "The New Pharmacy and Its Influences." *Bulletin of Pharmacy 15* (5):196- 200.
_____. (1901c). "The New Pharmacy and Its Influences [continued from *15* (5)]."*Bulletin of Pharmacy 15* (6): 242-3.
_____. (1901d). *Bulletin of Pharmacy 15* (1): 12-3.
_____. (1903). "An Anti-narcotic Law." *Proceedings of the American Pharmaceutical Association 51*: 478-83.
_____. (1904). "The APhA and the NARD." *Bulletin of Pharmacy 18* (11): 466-8.
_____. (1905a). "The Mission of the APhA." *Bulletin of Pharmacy 19*: 422-5.
_____. (1905b). "A Debate on the Preservative Question." *Bulletin of Pharmacy 19*: 497-8.
_____. (1907). "The Conference of Pharmaceutical Faculties." *Bulletin of Pharmacy 21*: 489-99.
_____. (1910). *Common Poisons and Their Antidotes and Dose Tables*. Scio, OH: The Standard Institute of Pharmacy.
_____. (1915). "Relations of the United States Pharmacopoeia to the Law and the General Public." *Pharmaceutical Era 48* (1): 7-9.
_____. (1916). "A Plea for Sanity in Drug Regulation." *Journal of the American Pharmaceutical Association 5*: 1251.
_____. (1920). "Legislation: Rational and Irrational." *Pharmaceutical Era 53* (12): 357-60.
_____. (1926). "The Limitations upon the Political Machinery as a Cure for Economic and Social Ills." *American Druggist*, November.
_____. (1937). "The American Pharmaceutical Association as a Factor in American Food and Drug Regulation." *Journal of the American Pharmaceutical Association 26*: 747-51.
Beauregard, E. E. (1993). "The Beals: A Father and Son Devoted to Pharmacy." *Pharmacy in History 35* (1): 25-32.
Bender, G. A. (1981)."Henry Hurd Rusby—Scientific Explorer, Social Crusader, Scholastic Innovator." *Pharmacy in History 23*: 71-85.
Berridge, V. (1990). "Opium and the Doctors: Disease Theory and Policy." In *Lectures on the History of Psychiatry*, R. M. Murray and T. H. Turner (eds.). London: Gaskell Royal College of Psychiatrists.
Berridge, V., and Rawson, N. S. B. (1979). "Opiate Use and Legislative Control." *Social Science and Medicine 13* (3): 351-63.
Binswanger, H. (1990). *The Biological Basis of Teleological Concepts*, Los Angeles: Ayn Rand Institute Press.
Blake, J. B. (ed.). (1970). "Safeguarding the Public: Historical Aspects of Medicinal Drug Control." *Conference on the History of Medicinal Drug Control, National Library of Medicine*, 1968. Baltimore: The Johns Hopkins Press.
Booth, M. (1996). *Opium: A History*. London: Simon and Schuster.
Bottoms, A. (1995). "The Philosophy and Politics of Punishment and Sentencing." In *The Politics of Sentencing Reform*, C. Clarkson and R. Morgan (eds.). Oxford: Clarendon Press.

Brandt, A. M. (1987). *No Magic Bullet: A Social History of Venereal Disease in the United States Since 1880*. New York: Oxford University Press.

Brannon, M. (1984). *Organizing and Reorganizing FDA. Seventy-fifth Anniversary Commemorative Volume of Food and Drug Law*. Washington, DC: Food and Drug Law Institute.

Brock, W. R. (1984). *Investigation and Responsibility: Public Responsibility in the United States, 1865-1900*. New York: Cambridge University Press.

Brown, E. R. (1979). *Rockefeller Medicine Men: Medicine and Capitalism in America*. Berkeley: University of California Press.

Buerki, R. A. (1999). "In Search of Excellence: The First Century of the American Association of Colleges of Pharmacy." *American Journal of Pharmaceutical Education 63*: 17-46 (Fall Supplement).

Burkholder, D. F. (1968). "Martin Inventius Wilbert (1865-1916): Hospital Pharmacist, Historian, and Scientist." *American Journal of Hospital Pharmacy 25*, 330-343, KRF, A2: Wilbert, Martin Inventius, Folder 3.

Campbell, B. C. (1980). *Representative Democracy: Public Policy and Midwestern Legislatures in the Late Nineteenth Century*. Cambridge: Harvard University Press.

Carr, E. H. (1961). *What is History?* New York: Vintage Books.

Cavallito, C. J. (1979). "Effects of Scheduling on the Economics of Drug Development." *NIDA Research Monograph 27*: 17-28.

Cavers, D. B. (1970). "The Evolution of the Contemporary System of Drug Regulation under the 1938 Act." In *Safeguarding the Public: Historical Aspects of Medicinal Drug Control*, J. B. Blake (ed.). Baltimore: The Johns Hopkins Press.

Christensen, C. N. (1978). "Federal Regulation: Philosophy and Practice." *Annals of Internal Medicine 89* (5): 835-7.

Christopher, T. W. (1958). "Articles on Food and Drug Law." *Food Drug and Cosmetic Law Journal 13*: 487-98.

Cipolle, R. J., Strand, L. M., and Morley, P. C. (1998). *Pharmaceutical Care Practice*. New York: McGraw-Hill.

Clancy, C. M. and Eisenberg, J. M. (1998). "Outcomes Research: Measuring the End Results of Health Care." *Science 282*: 245-6.

Collins, F. S., Patrinos, A., Jordan, E. et al. (1998). "New Goals for the U.S. Human Genome Project: 1998-2003." *Science 282*: 682-9.

Cowen, D. L. (1942). "America's First Pharmacy Laws." *Journal of the American Pharmaceutical Association Practical Pharmacy Edition 3*: 162-69, 214-21.

_____. (1943). "Louisiana, Pioneer in the Regulation of Pharmacy." *Louisiana Historical Quarterly 26* (2): 330-40.

_____. (1964). "Pharmacy as a Reflection of Cultures." *Chemist and Druggist* 12 December: 593-4.

_____. (1969.) "Liberty, Laissez-faire, and Licensure in Nineteenth-Century Britain." *Bulletin of the History of Medicine 43*: 30-40.

_____. (1982). "Robert P. Fischelis, 1891-1981." *New Jersey Journal of Pharmacy* February: 12-14.

_____. (1984). "Pharmacy and Freedom." *American Journal of Hospital Pharmacy 41*: 459-67.

_____. (1992). "Pharmacists and Physicians: An Uneasy Relationship." *Pharmacy in History 34* (1): 3-16.

Cowen, D. L., and Helfand, W. H. (1979). "The Progressive Movement and Its Impact on Pharmacy." *Pharmaceutica Acta Helvetiae 11*.

Crout, J. R. (1981). "The Drug Regulatory System: Reflections and Predictions." *Drug Intelligence and Clinical Pharmacy 15*: 793-8.

Cummings, H. S. (1929). "The Pharmacist in Relation to Public Health." *Pharmaceutical Era 66* (1): 13-4.

_____. (1929). "The Pharmacist in Relation to Public Health (part 2)." *Pharmaceutical Era 66* (2): 47-8.

Dally, A. (1995). "Anomalies and Mysteries in the 'War on Drugs'." In *Drugs and Narcotics in History*, R. Porter and M. Teich (eds.). Cambridge: Cambridge University Press.

Department of the Treasury, United States Public Health Service. (1906). General Comments 1. Legal Status and Development 1. Pure Food and Drug Law. *Digest of Comments of the Pharmacopoeia of the United States of America VII, and on the National Formulary-III 1*: 17-90.

Dibble, V. (1963). "Four Types of Inference from Documents to Events." *History and Theory 3*: 203-21.

Diehl, C. L. (1903). "Report on the Progress of Pharmacy." *Proceedings of the American Pharmaceutical Association 51*: 447-530, 568-577.

_____. (1904). "Minutes of the Section on Education and Legislation." *Proceedings of the American Pharmaceutical Association 52*: 93-184, 453-464.

_____. (1905). "Minutes of the Section on Education and Legislation." *Proceedings of the American Pharmaceutical Association 53*: 103-173, 474-482.

_____. (1906). "Report on the Progress of Pharmacy." *Proceedings of the American Pharmaceutical Association 54*: 159-173, 564-77.

_____. (1907). "Report on the Progress of Pharmacy." *Proceedings of the American Pharmaceutical Association 56*: 603-11.

_____. (1912). "Pharmacy—General Subjects." *APhA Yearbook*.

_____. (1913). "Report on the Progress of Pharmacy." *Proceedings of the American Pharmaceutical Association 62*: 1-7.

DiMasi, J. A., Hansen, R. W., Grabowski, H. G. et al. (1991). "Cost of Innovation in the Pharmaceutical Industry." *Journal of Health Economics 10*: 107-42.

Dingeslstad, D. et al. (1996). "The Social Construction of Drug Debates." *Social Science and Medicine 43*(12): 1829-38.

Dowling, H. F. (1971). *Medicines for Man: The Development, Regulation, and Use of Prescription Drugs*. New York: Alfred A. Knopf.

Dupree, A. H. (1962). Comment. In *The Government and The Consumer: Evolution of Food and Drug Laws*, J. L. Bates (ed.). Chicago: American Historical Association, 39-42.

_____. (1957). *Science in the Federal Government: A History of Policies and Activities to 1940.* Cambridge, MA: Belknap Press of Harvard University Press.

Durkheim, E. (1966). *The Rules of Sociological Method,* 8th edition. G. E. G. Catlin (ed.), Sarah A. Solovay and John H. Mueller (trans.). New York: Free Press.

Eccles, R.G. (1905). "A Debate on the Preservative Question." *Bulletin of Pharmacy 19*: 498-9.

England, J. W. (1908). "Address of the Chairman of the Section on Education and Legislation." *Proceedings of the American Pharmaceutical Association 56*: 602-5.

Evans, W. E. ,and Relling, M. V. (1999). "Pharmacogenomics: Translating Functional Genomics into Rational Therapeutics." *Science 286*: 487-91.

Fairchild, A. L., and Bayer, R. (1999). "Uses and Abuses of Tuskegee." *Science 284*: 919-21.

Fay, P. W. (1997). *The Opium War: 1840-1842.* Chapel Hill: The University of North Carolina Press.

Fischelis, R. P. (1930a). "Legal and Moral Obligations." *Pharmaceutical Era 67* (12): 353-4.

_____. (1930b). "Guarding the Purity of Drugs." *Pharmaceutical Era 67*(11): 320.

_____. (1931). "A Survey of State Pharmacy Laws with Reference to the Sale of Drugs and Medicines by General Merchants." *Journal of the American Pharmaceutical Association 20* (12): 1331-1341.

Food and Drug Administration. (1951). *Federal Food, Drug and Cosmetic Law: Administrative Reports, 1907-1949.* Chicago: Commerce Clearing House.

Forbes, J. W. (1910). "Who Owns the Prescription?" *Proceedings of the American Pharmaceutical Association 58*: 673-679.

Fox, D. M. (1991). "History of Drug Use and Drug Control." *Mount Sinai Journal of Medicine 58* (5): 403-5.

Fuchs, V. (1974). *Who Shall Live? Health, Economics, and Social Choice.* New York: Basic Books.

Fuller, B. P., Ellis, M. J., Barr, P. A. et al. (1999). "Privacy in Genetic Research." *Science 285*: 1359-61.

Gates, O. H. (1934). *Decisions of Courts in Cases under the Federal Food and Drugs Act.* Washington, DC: Office of the Solicitor, U.S. Department of Agriculture.

Glover, M. W. (1920). "The Administration of the Sherley Amendment." *F&D Review 4* (October): 17-9.

Good, B. J. (1994). *Medicine, Rationality, and Experience: An Anthropological Perspective.* Cambridge: Cambridge University Press.

Grabowski, H. G., and Vernon, J. M. (1983). *The Regulation of Pharmaceuticals: Balancing the Benefits and Risks.* Washington, DC: American Enterprise Institute for Public Policy Research.

Greely, H. T. (1998). "Legal, Ethical, and Social Issues in Human Genome Research." *Annual Review of Anthropology 27*: 473-502.

Griffenhagen, G. B., Blockstein, W. L., and Krigstein, D. J. (eds. (1994). "1919 Remington Medallist—James Hartley Beal (1861-1945)" and "1930 Remington Medallist—Edward Kremers (1865-1941)." In *The Remington Lectures: A Century in American Pharmacy.* Washington, DC: American Pharmaceutical Association, 11-15 and 53-57.

Hamit, H. F. (1975). "Tyranny of Standards." *Journal of the American Medical Association 233* (3): 226-7.

Harrison Anti-narcotic Act. (1914).

Hayes, A. H. (1981). "Food and Drug Regulation after 75 Years." *Journal of the American Medical Association 246* (11): 1223-6.

Herty, C. H. (1919). *The Future Independence and Progress of American Medicine in the Age of Chemistry.* J. J. Abel, C. L. Alsberg, R. F. Bacon, F. R. Eldred, R. Hunt, T. B. Johnson, J. Stieglitz, F .O. Taylor (eds.). The Chemical Foundation.

Helfand, W. H. (1975). "The United States and International Drug Regulatory Approaches." *Journal of the American Pharmaceutical Association NS15* (12):702-4.

Higby, G. J. (ed.) (1989). *One Hundred Years of the National Formulary*, Madison, WI: American Institute of the History of Pharmacy).

_____. (1992). *In Service to American Pharmacy: The Professional Life of William Proctor, Jr.* Tuscaloosa: The University of Alabama.

Higby, G. J., and Stroud, E. C. (1995). *The History of Pharmacy: A Selected Annotated Bibliography.* New York: Garland Publishing, Inc.

_____ (eds.). (1997). *The Inside Story of Medicines: A Symposium.* Madison, WI: American Institute of the History of Pharmacy.

Hiss, A. E. (1898). *Thesaurus of Proprietary Preparation and Pharmaceutical Specialties: Including "Patent" Medicines, Proprietary Pharmaceuticals, Open-formula Specialties, Synthetic Remedies, etc.* Chicago: Englehard and Company.

Hoak, R. D. (1958). "A Farewell to Dr. [George] Beal." *Mellon Institute News*, 17 July: 1-7.

Hofstadter, R. (1955). *The Age of Reform: From Bryan to F.D.R.* New York: Vantage Books.

_____ (ed.). (1986). *The Progressive Movement, 1900 to 1915.* New York: Touchstone Books, Simon & Shuster.

Hook, G. B., and Beal, G. D. (n.d.). "The Life and Character of James Hartley Beal." Pittsburgh: Mellon Institute, KFR, A2: J. H. Beal.

Hopkins, R. J. (1965). "Medical Prescriptions and the Law." Masters thesis, Emory University.

Hoover, H. (1924). "Associations Vital to Modern Business: Standards of Commerce Should Be Developed by Those Affected." *Pharmaceutical Era 58* (19): 443-4.

Hunt, E. M. (1877). "The Relations of the Pharmacist to the Medical Profession." In *Transactions of the International Medical Congress*, John Ashhurst (ed.). Philadelphia: Centennial Medical Commission of Philadelphia.

Humphreys, M. (1992). *Yellow Fever and the South.* New Brunswick, NJ: Rutgers University Press.

Hutt, P. B. (1985). "The Importance of Analytical Chemistry to Food and Drug Regulation." *Journal of the Association of Official Analytical Chemists* 8 (2): 147-51.

Hutt, P. B., and Merrill, R. A. (1991). *Food and Drug Law: Cases and Materials.* Westbury, NY: Foundation Press.

Illich, I. (1976). *Medical Nemesis.* New York: Random House.

Interstate Commerce Act. (1887).

Jackson, C. O. (1970). *Food and Drug Legislation in the New Deal.* Princeton, NJ: Princeton University Press.

Janssen, W. F. (1964). "FDA since 1938: The Major Trends and Developments." *Journal of Public Law 13* (1): 205-21.

_____. (1981). "Pharmacy and the Food and Drug Law." *American Pharmacy NS21* (4): 28-36.

_____. (1981). "The Story of the Laws Behind the Labels." *FDA Consumer 15* (5): 32-45.

Johnson, J. A., and Bootman, J. L. (1995). "Drug-related Morbidity and Mortality: A Cost-of-illness Model." *Archives of Internal Medicine 155* (18): 1949-56.

Johnson vs. United States, 221 U.S. 488. (1911).

Kallet, A., and Schlink, F. J. (1933). *100,000,000 Guinea Pigs: Dangers in Everyday Foods, Drugs, and Cosmetics.* New York: Vanguard Press.

Kantor, A. F. (1976). "Upton Sinclair and the Pure Food and Drugs Act of 1906." *American Journal of Public Health 66* (12): 1202-5.

Kauffman, G. B. (1905). "President James H. Beal." *Bulletin of Pharmacy 19*: 185-7.

Kauffman, N. M., Malevich, S., Smith, D. J. et al. (1980). "Food and Drug Administration part 1: Federal Agency Close-up." *American Journal of Medical Technology 46* (6): 428-36.

Kebler, L. F. (1909). *Drug Legislation in the United States Revised to July 15, 1908.* Washington, DC: US Department of Agriculture, Bureau of Chemistry.

_____. (1912). "U.S.P. as a Standard." *Journal of the American Medical Association 59*: 1165.

_____. (1930). "The Work of Three Pioneers in Initiating Food and Drug Legislation." *Journal of the American Pharmaceutical Association 19*: 59-96.

Kennedy, D. (1981). "Regulation and the Health Professions." *Mobius 1* (1): 36-46.

King, N. M. (1987). *A Selection of Primary Sources for the History of Pharmacy in the United States.* Madison, WI: American Institute of the History of Pharmacy.

Kleinfeld, V. A. (1995). "Legislative History of the Federal Food, Drug, and Cosmetic Act." *Food and Drug Law Journal 50*: 65-99.

Knoppers, B. M., Hirtle, M., and Glass, K. C. (1999). "Commercialization of Genetic Research and Public Policy." *Science 286*: 2277-8.

Kondratas, R. A. (1982). "Biologics Control Act of 1902." In *The Early Years of the Federal Food and Drug Control*, J. H. Young (ed.). Madison, WI: American Institute of the History of Pharmacy.

Korwck, E. L. (1982). "FDA, OSHA, and EPA Regulation of the Recombinant DNA Technology." *Journal of Parenteral Science and Technology 36* (6): 251-5.

Kremers, E. (1907). "Reading the Signs of the Times." *Bulletin of Pharmacy 21*: 64-6.

_____. (1940). "The History of American Pharmacy." In *Introductory Essays on the History of Pharmacy*, J. J. Corcoran (ed.). Minneapolis, MN: Burgess Publishing.

Lamb, R. (1936). *American Chamber of Horror: The Truth about Food and Drugs*. New York: Farrar and Rinehart.

LaWall, C. (1908). "Minutes of the Fifty-Sixth Annual Meeting." *Proceedings of the American Pharmaceutical Association 56*: 143, 469-470, 602-5.

_____. (1919). "Bolshevism in Pharmacy." *Pharmaceutical Era 52* (1): 7-9.

_____. (1929). "What Professional Pharmacy Can Do for Medicine and What It May Expect in Return." *International Clinics 2*: 244-52.

Liebenau, J. M. (1981). "Medical Science and Medical Industry, 1980-1929: A Study of Pharmaceutical Manufacturers in Philadelphia." Ph.D. diss., University of Pennsylvania.

Link, A. S. (1954). *Woodrow Wilson and the Progressive Era, 1910-1917*. New York: Harper and Row.

Linton, F.B. (1995) "Federal Food and Drug Laws—Leaders Who Achieved Their Enactment and Enforcement." *Food and Drug Law Journal 50*: 9-58.

Lloyd, J. U. (1920). "When is Poison Not a Poison?" *Pharmaceutical Era 53* (12): 361-2.

Longest, Jr., B. B. (1998). *Health Policymaking in the United States*. Chicago: Health Administration Press.

Maisch, J. M. (1868). *Report on the Legislation Regulating the Practice of Pharmacy in the United States*. Philadelphia: Merrihew and Son, Printers, cited in King.

Marks, H. M. (1987). "Ideas as Reforms: Therapeutic Experiments and Medical Practice, 1900-1980." Ph.D. diss., Massachusetts Institute of Technology.

Marks, H. M. (1997). *The Progress of Experiment: Science and Therapeutic Reform in the United States, 1900-1990*. Cambridge: Cambridge University Press.

Marshall, G. (1994). *The Concise Oxford Dictionary of Sociology*. Oxford: Oxford University Press.

Mason, H. B. (1901). "Edward Kremers." *Bulletin of Pharmacy 15* (5): 150-1.

_____. (1907). "Are the Colleges in Harmony with Present Conditions?" *Bulletin of Pharmacy 21*: 401-2.

McGinnis, F. S. (1944). "The History of the Development of Drug Standards in the United States." Ph.D. diss., University of Pittsburgh.

Melton, G. B., and M. J. Saks. (1985). "The Law as an Instrument of Socialization and Social Structure." *Nebraska Symposium on Motivation 33*: 235-77.

Mises, L. (1949). *Human Action: A Treatise on Economics*. San Francisco: Fox and Wilkes.

Molseed, C. S. (1930). "The Physician and Pharmacist: Closer Cooperation Between the Two Professions Would Benefit Both, and Each Practitioner Should Stay in His Own Field." *Pharmaceutical Era 67* (9): 261-2.

Moreno, J. (1999). *Undue Risk: State Experiments on Humans*. New York: Freeman.

Morgan, H. W. (1981). *Drugs in America*. Syracuse, NY: Syracuse University Press.

Morgan, R., and Clarkson, C. (eds.). (1995). *The Politics of Sentencing Reform*. Oxford: Clarendon Press.

Moros, D. A. (1991). "Drug Use: Social and Scientific Background." *Mount Sinai Journal of Medicine 58* (5): 437-40.

Musto, D. (1987). *The American Disease: Origins of Narcotic Control*. New York: Oxford University Press.

Musto, D. F. (1991). "Opium, Cocaine, and Marijuana in American History." *Scientific American 265* (1): 40-7.

Nelson, C. F. (1917). "The Pharmacist and the State: Are Certificate Renewals a Necessity?" *Pharmaceutical Era 50* (2): 50-1.

Numbers, R. L. (1987). "The Fall and Rise of the American Medical Profession." In *Sickness and Health in America: Readings in the History of Medicine and Public Health*, J. W. Leavitt and R. L. Numbers (eds.). Madison: University of Wisconsin Press.

Ogier, W. R. (1903). "Making a Profession by Law." *Proceedings of the American Pharmaceutical Association 51*: 526-8.

Okun, M. (1986). *Fair Play in the Marketplace: The First Battle for Pure Food*. DeKalb, IL: Northern Illinois University Press.

Oliker, L. R. (1965). "Pharmaceutical Industry; Institutional Characteristics and Statutory Review." DBA thesis, Indiana University.

O'Reilly, J. T. (1993). *Food and Drug Administration*. Colorado Springs, CO: Shepard's McGraw-Hill.

Patton, J. F. (1903). "Practical Education." *Proceedings of the American Pharmaceutical Association 51*: 528-9.

Parascandola, J. (1992). *The Development of American Pharmacology: John J. Abel and the Shaping of a Discipline*. Baltimore: The Johns Hopkins University Press.

_____. (1994). "Pharmacology and Public Health: The Jamaica Ginger Paralysis Episode of the 1930s." *Pharmacy in History 36*: 123-31.

_____. (1995). "The Drug Habit: The Association of the Word 'Drug' with Abuse in American History." In *Drugs and Narcotics in History*, R. Porter and M. Teich (eds.). Cambridge: Cambridge University Press.

_____. (1997). "Alkaloids to Arsenicals: Systematic Drug Discovery Before the First World War." In *The Inside Story of Medicines: A Symposium*, G. J. Higby and E. C. Stroud (eds.). Madison, WI, American Institute of the History of Pharmacy, 77-91.

Parrish II, R. H. (1985a). "Defining Liberty [letter]." *American Journal of Hospital Pharmacy 42*: 1711-2.

_____. (1985b). "Drug Distribution and Government Intervention [letter]." *merican Pharmacy NS25* (11): 653-4.

Parrish II, R. H., and Parrish, M. (1983). "3:29 a.m." *American Journal of Hospital Pharmacy 40*: 861-3.

Penn, R. G. (1979). "The State Control of Medicines: The First 3000 Years." *British Journal of Clinical Pharmacology 8*: 293-305.

Podolsky, M. L. (1997). *Cures Out of Chaos: How Unexpected Discoveries Led to Breakthroughs in Medicine and Health.* Amsterdam: Overseas Publishers Association.

Ponthieu, M. G. (1902). "Standardization." *Bulletin of Pharmacy 16* (1): 23-5.

Porter, R. (1997). *The Greatest Benefit to Mankind: A Medical History of Humanity.* New York: W.W. Norton & Co.

Post Office Regulation 17 Stat 322-23 (1872).

Poovey, M. (1998). *The History of the Modern Fact: Problems of Knowledge in the Sciences of Wealth and Society.* Chicago: University of Chicago Press.

Pub. L. 59-384, 34 Stat. 786. (1906).

Pub. L. 75-717, 21 U.S.C. 301-392. (1938).

Randall, F. D. (1972). "Corporate Strategies in the Drug Industry: A Study of Strategic Response to Social and Political Pressures." DBA thesis, Harvard University.

Risse, G. B. (1997). "The Road to Twentieth-Century Therapeutics: Shifting Perspectives and Approaches." In *The Inside Story of Medicines: A Symposium*, G. J. Higby and E. C. Stroud (eds.). Madison, WI: American Institute of the History of Pharmacy.

Robinson-Patman Act 15 U.S. C. § 13a, 13b, 21a. (1937).

Rosen, G. (1953). "Cameralism and the Concept of Medical Police." *Bulletin of the History of Medicine 27*: 21-41.

Rosenberg, C. (1979). "The Therapeutic Revolution: Medicine, Meaning, and Social Change in Nineteenth-Century America." In *The Therapeutic Revolution*, C. Rosenberg and M. Vogel (eds.). Philadelphia: University of Pennsylvania Press.

Rusby, H. H. (1927). "Pharmacopoeia for Safety of People." *Pharmaceutical Era 64* (4): 97-100.

_____. (1928). "Bureaucracy, 'Regulations' and the Law." *Pharmaceutical Era 64* (12): 47-8.

Russell, J. C. H. (1946). "The Interrelationship of Pharmacy and Medicine." *American Journal of Pharmaceutical Education 10*: 286-312.

Savitt, T. L., and Young, J. H. (eds.). (1988). *Disease and Distinctiveness in the American South.* Knoxville: University of Tennessee Press.

Schmeckebier, L. F., and Eble, F. X. A. (1923). *The Bureau of Internal Revenue: Its History, Activities, and Organization.* Baltimore: The Johns Hopkins Press.

Sherley amendment, 37 Stat. 416. (1912).

Sherman Act 15 U.S.C. §§ 1-7. (1890).

Shorter, E. (1987). *The Health Century.* New York: Doubleday.

Silverman, M., and Lee, P. R. (1974). *Pills, Profits, and Politics.* Berkeley: University of California Press.

Silverson, R. (1988). *Register of Edward Kremers (1865-1941).* Madison: Wisconsin Historical Society.

Simmons, G. (1905). "The Secret Nostrum vs. the Ethical Proprietary Preparations." *Journal of the American Medical Association 44*: 718-21.

Skinner, W. J. (1980)."Freedom of Speech and Freedom of the Press in Medical and Pharmacy Practice." *Drug Intelligence and Clinical Pharmacy 14*: 609-16.

Skocpol, T. (1992). *Protecting Soldiers and Mothers: The Political Origins of Social Policy in the United States.* Cambridge, MA: The Belknap Press of Harvard University Press.

_____. (1995). "Why I Am an Historical Institutionalist." *Polity 28*: 103-6.

Sletten, C. (1959). "The Social Structure and Ideology of Organized Pharmacy: With Special Reference to Price Competition." Ph.D. diss., Harvard University.

Sneader, W. (1985). *Drug Discovery: The Evolution of Modern Medicines.* New York: John Wiley & Sons Ltd.

Sonnedecker, G. A. (1970). "Contribution of the Pharmaceutical Profession toward Controlling the Quality of Drugs in the Nineteenth Century." In *Safeguarding the Public: Historical Aspects of Medicinal Drug Control,* J. B. Blake (ed.). Baltimore, MD: The Johns Hopkins Press.

_____. (1953). "The Section on Education and Legislation of the American Pharmaceutical Association." *American Journal of Pharmaceutical Education 17*: 362-83.

_____. (1982). "Drug Standards Become Official." In *The Early Years of the Federal Food and Drug Control,* J. II. Young (ed.). Madison, WI: American Institute of the History of Pharmacy.

_____. (1986). *Kremers and Urdang's History of Pharmacy.* Madison, WI: American Institute of the History of Pharmacy.

Sonnedecker, G. A., and Urdang, G. (1953). "Legalization of Drug Standards Under State Laws in the United States of America." *Food Drug and Cosmetic Law Journal 8* (12): 741-60.

Starr, P. (1982). *The Social Transformation of American Medicine: The Rise of a Sovereign Profession and the Making of a Vast Industry.* New York: Basic Books.

Stewart, F. E. (1901). "Proposed National Bureau of Materia Medica." *Journal of the American Medical Association,* April 27: 1177.

_____. (1903). "Report of F. E. Stewart, as Committee of One Appointed for the Purpose of Transmitting the Views of the American Pharmaceutical Association on the Subject of Patents and Trademarks to the Congress of the United States of America." *Proceedings of the American Pharmaceutical Association 51*: 463-6.

_____. (1917). "The Biologicals of the U.S. Pharmacopoeia." *Pharmaceutical Era 50* (1): 9-11.

_____. (1917). "The Biologicals of the U.S. Pharmacopoeia: How Vaccines and Antitoxins are Officially Treated. *Pharmaceutical Era 50* (2): 47-9.

Stieb, E. W. (1966). *Drug Adulteration: Detection and Control in Nineteenth-Century Britain.* Madison: The University of Wisconsin Press.

Strong, H. R. (1912). "The Richardson Bill Dead." *National Druggist 42*: 333.

Swallow, E. (1925). "Liquor as a Therapeutic Agent." *Pharmaceutical Era 59* (7): 3-4.

Swann, J. P. (1988). *Academic Scientists and the Pharmaceutical Industry: Cooperative Research in Twentieth-Century America*. Baltimore: The Johns Hopkins University Press.

_____. (1994). "FDA and the Practice of Pharmacy: Prescription Drug Regulation to 1951." *Pharmacy in History 36*: 55-70.

Szasz, T. S. (1992). *Our Right to Drugs: The Case for a Free Market*. New York: Praeger.

Temin, P. (1980). *Taking Your Medicine: Drug Regulation in the United States*. Cambridge: Harvard University Press.

_____. (1983). "Costs and Benefits in Switching Drugs from Prescription to Over-the-Counter." *Journal of Health Economics 2*: 187-205.

Terry, C. E., and Pellens, M. (1928). *The Opium Problem*. New York: The Bureau of Social   Hygiene.

Turner, B. S. (1987). *Medical Power and Social Knowledge*. London: Sage Publications.

United States Constitution.

Waley, A. (1958). *The Opium War Through Chinese Eyes*. Stanford, CA: Stanford University Press.

Walker III, W. O. (1981). *Drug Control in the Americas*. Albuquerque: University of New Mexico Press.

Wardell, W. M., and Lasagna, L. (1975). *Regulation and Drug Development*. Washington, DC: American Enterprise Institute for Public Policy Research.

Watts, S. (1997). *Epidemics and History: Disease, Power, and Imperialism*. New Haven, CT: Yale University Press.

Weatherford, J. (1997). *The History of Money: From Sandstone to Cyberspace*. New York: Three Rivers Press.

Wedderburn, A. J. (1894). *A Compilation of the Pharmacy and Drug Laws of the Several States and Territories*. Washington, DC: US Department of Agriculture, Division of Chemistry.

Wiebe, R. H. (1962). *Businessmen and Reform: A Study of the Progressive Movement*. Cambridge, MA: Harvard University Press.

_____. (1967). *The Search For Order, 1877-1920*. New York: Hull and Wang.

_____. (1975). *The Segmented Society: An Introduction to the Meaning of America*. New York: Oxford University Press.

_____. (1995). *Self-Rule: A Cultural History of American Democracy*. Chicago: University of Chicago Press.

Wilbert, M. I. (1904). "The Pharmacist and the Physician: A New Aspect of the Case." *Proceedings of the American Pharmaceutical Association 52*: 150-3.

_____. (1913a). "The National Formulary and Proprietary Remedies." *Pharmaceutical   Era 46*: 547.

_____. (1913b). "Poisons and Habit-forming Drugs: A Digest of Laws and Regulations Relating to the Possession, Use, Sale, and Manufacture of Poisons and Habit-forming Drugs Enacted during 1912 and 1913, Now in Force in the United States." *Public Health Reports 27* (41) and (42), KRF, A2: Wilbert, Martin Inventius, Folder 2.

_____. (1914). "Pure Drugs and the Public Health." *Public Health Reports 29* (19), KRF, A2: Wilbert, Martin Inventius, Folder 2.

_____. (1915a). "The Limitations of Self-Medication: Uses and Abuses of Proprietary Preparations and Household Remedies." *Public Health Reports 30* (7), KRF, A2: Wilbert, Martin Inventius, Folder 2.

_____. (1915b). "Drug Intoxication: An Economic Waste and a Menace to Public Health." *Pharmaceutical Era 48* (2): 55-7.

Wilbert, M. I. and Motter, M. G. (1912). *Digest of Laws and Regulations in Force in the United States Relating to the Possession, Use, Sale, and Manufacture of Poisons and Habit-Forming Drugs.* Washington, DC: United States Public Health Service.

Wiley, H. R. (1904). *A Treatise on Pharmaceutical Jurisprudence with a Thesis on the Law in General.* San Francisco: The Hicks-Judd Co.

Wiley, H. W. (1905). "A Debate on the Preservative Question." *Bulletin of Pharmacy 19*: 499-501.

_____. (1929). *History of a Crime Against the Food Law.* New York: de Vinne-Hallenbeck Company.

_____. (1930). *An Autobiography.* Indianapolis, IN: Bobbs-Merrill.

Williams, R. J. (1884). *A View of the Laws Relating to Physicians, Druggists, and Dentists.* Philadelphia: William P. Kildare, printer (Cowen Reference Files).

Wilson, J. Q. (1990). "Drugs and Crime." In *Drugs and Crime*, M. Tonry and J. Q. Wilson (eds.). Chicago: The University of Chicago Press.

Wood, H. C. (1929). "What Can the Medical Profession Do for Pharmacy?" *International Clinics 2*: 237-43.

Wolfe, M. R. (1978). *Lucias Brown Polk and Progressive Food and Drug Control: Tennessee and New York City, 1908-1920.* Lawrence: Regents Press of Kansas.

Young, J. H. (1959). "The Origin of Patent Medicines in America." *Chemist and Druggist*, September 9: 9-16.

_____. (1961a). "American Medical Quackery in the Age of the Common Man." *Mississippi Historical Review 47* (4): 579-93.

_____. (1961b). *The Toadstool Millionaires: A Social History of Patent Medicines in American before Federal Regulation.* Princeton, NJ: Princeton University Press.

_____. (1964a). "The Government and the Consumer: Evolution of Food and Drug Laws. The 1938 Food, Drug, and Cosmetic Act." *Journal of Public Law 13*: 197-204.

_____. (1964b). "Social History of American Drug Regulation." In *Drugs in Our Society*, P. Talalay (ed.). Baltimore: The Johns Hopkins Press, 217-9.

_____. (1965). "The American Drug Scene." *Emory University Quarterly 21*: 71-141.

_____. (1967). *The Medical Messiahs: A Social History of Health Quackery in Twentieth Century America.* Princeton, NJ: Princeton University Press.

_____. (1968). "The Science and Morals of Metabolism: Catsup and Benzoate of Soda." *Journal of the History of Medicine and Allied Sciences 23* (1).

_____. (1970). "Drugs and the 1906 Law." In *Safeguarding the Public: Historical Aspects of Medicinal Drug Control*, J. B. Blake (ed.). Baltimore: The Johns Hopkins Press.

_____. (1974a). *American Self-Dosage Medicines: An Historical Perspective.* Lawrence, KS: Cioronado Press.

_____. (1974b). "Saccharin: A Bitter Regulatory Controversy." In *Research in the Administration of Public Policy*, F. B. Evans and H. T. Pinkett (eds.).Washington, DC: Howard University Press.

_____. (1980). "FDA Yesterday: Talk at Orientation of New FDA Scientists." Madison, WI: AIHP Reference Files (Cowen Reference Files).

_____. (1981a). "The Long Struggle for the 1906 Law." *FDA Consumer* June: 12-6.

_____. (1981b). "Self-Dosage Medicine in America: 1906 and 1981." *South Atlantic Quarterly 80* (4): 379.

_____. (1982a). "Public Policy and Drug Innovation." *Pharmacy in History 24*: 3-31.

_____ (ed.). (1982b). *The Early Years of Federal Food and Drug Control.* Madison, WI: American Institute of the History of Pharmacy.

_____. (1983a). "Food and Drug Administration." In *Government Agencies*, D. R. Whitnah (ed.). Westport, CT: Greenwood Press.

_____. (1983b). "Sulfanilamide and Diethylene Glycol." In *Chemistry and Modern Society: Historical Essays in Honor of Aaron J. Ihde*, J. Parascandola and J. C. Wharton (eds.). Washington, DC: American Chemical Society.

_____. (1983c). "Sulfanilamide and Diethylene Glycol." *Chemistry and Modern Society 6*: 106-25.

_____. (1983d). "Three Southern Food and Drug Cases." *Journal of Southern History 49* (1): 3-36.

_____. (1990). "Food and Drug Regulation under the USDA 1906-1940." *Agricultural History 64* (2): 134-42.

_____. (1989). *Pure Food: Securing the Federal Food and Drugs Act of 1906.* Princeton, NJ: Princeton University Press.

_____. (1992a). *American Health Quackery.* Princeton NJ: Princeton University Press.

_____. (1992b). "Food and Drug Enforcers in the 1920s: Restraining and Educating." *Business and Economic History 21*: 119-27.

Young, J. H., and Griffenhagen, G. B. (1959). *Old English Patent Medicines in America.* Washington, DC: Smithsonian Institution.

Primary Unpublished Bibliography

American Institute of the History of Pharmacy and F. B. Power Memorial Library, School of Pharmacy, University of Wisconsin, Madison, Wisconsin.
    Kremers Reference Files.
    Cowen Reference Files.
American Pharmaceutical Association Archives, Washington, DC.

American Social Hygiene Association Papers, Social Welfare History Archives
    Center, University of Minnesota, Minneapolis, Minnesota.
National Archives II, College Park, Maryland.
    RG 16, Department of Agriculture–1910-1938.
    RG 88, Food and Drug Administration and predecessors–1919-1938.
Wisconsin State Historical Archives, Madison, Wisconsin.
    National Association of Boards of Pharmacy Archives.
    Edward Kremers Papers.
    Francis E. Stewart Papers.
    Robert P. Fischelis Papers.

Index

Nostrums
    dangers of, 11-12
    government control of, 84
    legislative control of, 68
    narcotic contents of, 12
    secret formulas in, 12
    venereal disease treatment, 68
Nutritional supplements, FDA and, xi

Opium
    China use of, 19-20
    Philippines Island controlling, 18
    US use of, 19-20
    See also Narcotics

Parran, Thomas, 84
Patent medicines
    drug manufacturers and, 12-13
    federal government approaches, 12-
        13
    international narcotic control, 13-14
    nostrums and, 11-12
    physicians vs apothecaries clashes,
        11
    See also Drug manufacturing
Pharmaceutical Era, 51
Pharmaceutical fact
    compendia revisiting, 123
    as concept of consciousness, xxii
    defined, 31-32
    drug system dispensing, 120-121
    employment's effect, 41-43
    end use perspectives in, 116
    foundations for, 116
    government as arbiter, 118
    government commercial policies,
        116-119, 122-123
    individual practitioner determining,
        116
    as "modern fact," 39-41
    narcotic use control, 120
    negotiations in, xxii
    pharmaceutical characteristics, xxi-
        xxii
    pharmaceutical standard reasons,
        29-31
    pharmacopoeial scope, 32-39
    pharmacy's professional status, 119-
        120
    polity to policy, xxiii-xxiv
    practitioners roles, xxii-xxiii
    Progressive vs New Deal eras, 29

"pure" drug issues, 121
    quackery and, 121
    social control ideologies, 118
    standard's polity, 44-46
    therapy standards, 118
    venereal disease issues, 121-122
    worldview and, 44, 116
Pharmaceutical manufactures
    finished dose manufactures, 12
    professional vs public distribution, 13
    vs federal regulation enforcement, 13
Pharmaceutical Review, 53, 60
Pharmaceutical standards
    Campbell's thinking on, 105-107
    chemistry for, 91-92
    foreign origin therapies, 91
    industrial production and, 92
    National Formulary standards, 97-
        105
    organic pharmaceutical production,
        92
    phenol manufacturing, 91-92
    qualitative standards negotiating,
        107
    rubric enforcement problems, 92-
        95, 107, 122-123
    synthetic therapy production, 91-92
    variation allowing, 95-97
    See also Drug manufacturing
Pharmacists
    accountability of, 72
    ASHA regard for, 79
    ASHA survey fears of, 76-77
    Campbell on, 106
    exclusionary-type legislation, 5
    judgments lacking of, 81-82
    practice limits, 5-6
    professional status of, 119-120
    vs physicians, 32, 71-72, 83, 132
Pharmacopoeial scope
    areas of standardization, 33
    contents labels, 35-36
    drug control issues, 33-34
    government drug enforcement, 34-
        35
    healing approaches, 32
    physician and pharmacists organiz-
        ing, 32
Pharmazeutiche Rundschau, 53
Phelps, Francis M., 70
Power, F. B., 51
Proctor, William, 9, 33